Generous Influencers

Generous Influencers is an invitation to an abundant, prosperous life. Despite the tendency for success at the expense of others, Robert calls all into the endless possibilities unlocked when in service of others. Through a succinct simplicity, *Generous Influencers* manages to guide into the often-fraught waters of giving. Issues of personal wellness and boundaries are balanced with the continual call to give your best to the world. As one who knows Robert, his writing flows not from the abstract, but from the gregarious life he lives. I wholeheartedly endorse *Generous Influencers* and recommend it for all seeking to become a generous influencer!

— **Trevor William Horn,** Author of
The Art of Being: Finding Purpose in the Presence

In *Generous Influencers*, Robert Kaelin takes big helpings of his generous spirit and his big heart and mixes them together to pour out a practical and inspirational recipe for making a difference in the lives of the people around you. What comes out of the oven is a roadmap for embracing generosity and making a difference in your world. Robert uses stories, illustrations and practical tips to give you a new way to look at life and understand what it means to not only be successful, but also create significance and leave a lasting legacy of generosity and goodness. I recommend *Generous Influencers* to anyone who aspires to make a difference!

— **Karl J. Newman,** President & CEO,
WSRB/BuildingMetrix, Inc.

First of all, I have had the pleasure of knowing Robert Kaelin for only 3 or 4 years, but we connected quickly due to similarities in heart and vision. I so appreciate *Generous Influencers* because it is an introspective look into Robert's heart and motivation. His approach is practical and simple in its delivery, but very invasive if you are reading it to examine your life. Thank you, Robert, for taking the time to pen *Generous Influencers* and give us all an opportunity to reflect in the mirror of our own lives. God declares that 'we are created in His image' and as such, we are all called to live generously.

— **Dave Robbs,** Executive Director of the Poyeho Project

"Jesus Professed, "It is more blessed to give than to receive." Robert Kaelin teaches us why and how. *Generous Influencers* delivers a wonderfully defined command and call. Find purpose and practicality for development of character, the betterment of community, and the joy of loving others."

— **Jay Ward,** Co-Founder and
Creative Director at AdHatchery

Robert Kaelin's *Generous Influencers* book is timely for a culture increasingly steeped in narcissism and personal stinginess. He shows dramatically that a generous life is a good life that blesses both the giver and all those they touch. His insights and great stories will inspire you to be generous in all areas of your life, and help revive this important virtue in our families, neighborhoods, and culture."

— **Dr. Ron Boehme,** Youth With A Mission/
Faith International University

I met Robert Kaelin at a Live2Lead event my brother and I were hosting as a fundraising benefit with a local charity. Robert came up to me and introduced himself as so many people do. But he did one thing that was different from almost everyone else. He said we need to get together and he actually followed up. He owns a business in our community called Elements. I had never been to this frozen yogurt /coffee shop before my follow-up meeting with Robert. On the wall is a green neon sign that says, "Generous People". I asked him about it, and he stated, 'That is what Puyallup means, the land of Generous People.' That day. That conversation. It started a unique coaching, mentoring, and friendship with Robert, the author of *Generous Influencers*. I have watched him live out generosity and I have seen him grow as a leader in our community, being recognized for his efforts with a number of awards. Now as an author, he shares with you the key to impacting your community.

You are going to find *Generous Influencers* full of stories, many may be like your own, and see through the eyes of Robert, how to view life from a perspective of generosity to serve the people around you and the communities where you live. Robert challenges you, in a great way, to make a positive difference in your world, right where you are!

— **Mike Newman,** Founder and CEO
Innovations in Leadership

You Hold the Key to Creating a Positive Impact

Robert Kaelin

NEW YORK

LONDON • NASHVILLE • MELBOURNE • VANCOUVER

Generous Influencers

You Hold the Key to Creating a Positive Impact

Published in New York, New York, by Morgan James Publishing. Morgan James is a trademark of Morgan James, LLC. www.MorganJamesPublishing.com

Proudly distributed by Publishers Group West®

Scripture quotations and words of Jesus are taken or adapted from the New American Standard Bible, ® Copyright © 1960, 1962, 1963, 1968, 1971, 1973, 1975, 1977, 1995 by The Lockman Foundation. Used by permission.

Morgan James BOGO™

A **FREE** ebook edition is available for you or a friend with the purchase of this print book.

[ ]

CLEARLY SIGN YOUR NAME ABOVE

Instructions to claim your free ebook edition:
1. Visit MorganJamesBOGO.com
2. Sign your name CLEARLY in the space above
3. Complete the form and submit a photo of this entire page
4. You or your friend can download the ebook to your preferred device

ISBN 9781636981802 paperback
ISBN 9781636981819 ebook
Library of Congress Control Number:
2023934419

Cover & Interior Design by:
Christopher Kirk
www.GFSstudio.com

Editorial by:
Arlyn Lawrence,
Inspira Literary Solutions
Gig Harbor, Washington
www.inspiralit.com

Morgan James PUBLISHING **Builds** with... **Habitat for Humanity** Peninsula and Greater Williamsburg

Morgan James is a proud partner of Habitat for Humanity Peninsula and Greater Williamsburg. Partners in building since 2006.

Get involved today! Visit: www.morgan-james-publishing.com/giving-back

This book is dedicated to God,
who has shown me what generosity is,
and my family and community,
who have helped me learn how to practice and live it out daily:
Jackie, Robert, Lily, Sophia,
and Puyallup.

I LOVE YOU!

TABLE OF CONTENTS

ACKNOWLEDGMENTS

There are special people who show up in our lives and encourage us to accomplish our dreams. People who assist us in making them possible. To those people in my life, I want to acknowledge you here:

To God, who has given me life and saved me from a path of destruction and allowed me to experience the world in order to know Him better and be with Him forever.

To Jackie Kaelin, whose faith and positive support have allowed me to make a difference in the lives of others through living generously. Her example of generosity in our family has helped me to understand generosity in a meaningful way and allowed me to take those lessons and share them with others. Jackie, you are full of love, and I am thankful we get to partner in this adventurous life and positively impact others together.

To my children, who have supported their dad and given me the platform for my most important leadership practice as their father. They have humbled me and kept me on my toes. They have challenged my thinking and helped me to see there is so much love in this world.

To my parents, who have helped shape who I am and encouraged me to chase after my dreams. They have sacrificed much to allow me opportunities that helped me grow into the man I am today.

To my siblings, Jen, Tommy, Terrah, Dustin, and Shelby—beautiful people whom I love very much.

To Mike Newman, who many times caught the vision and helped me to get there, including this book and his generous contribution, especially to co-authoring chapter 8. Mike is a person who has added so much value to those who know him. He has been an inspiration, a mentor, someone I look up to and admire, a great friend, and someone who constantly sets the example of living generously.

To Arlyn Lawrence, my editor, my writing coach, and my friend who was able to challenge me when needed, help me process my thoughts, and deepened my understanding of true generosity. She showed up time after time to make this book what it is.

To my thought partners whom I would reach out to on a regular basis to help me process the thoughts contained in this book (in no particular order): Neil Hope, Kyle Rogers, Ruben Romero, Laura Romero, Chuck Valley, Travis Morris, John Kelley, Jonathan Waller, Trevor Horn, Jack Menashe, Robin McCoy, Kevin Barringer, Bryan Reynolds, Tara Doyle-Enneking, Jay Ward, Michaela Tews, Tony Frascone, Dave Robbs, Ron Pilo, Bill Bowers, Kyle Nelson, Rob Meyer, Nick Peterson, Luke Wilbanks, and Josh Shulkind.

Thank you for your contribution to making this book relate and come to life. Your friendship and partnership mean the world to me!

FOREWORD

Influence is big right now. It seems that everyone wants to be an influencer. And you can simply proclaim it as your profession, career, or job with no other qualifications. Set up a social media account. Bam. There you are. "I'm an influencer."

To be fair, it may be no different than declaring that you are a musician, a poet, or a business owner. However, a musician, poet, or business owner must make music, write poetry or sell a product or service. The audience or customer decides if there is value by trading their hard-earned money for what they receive.

Because the primary metrics for today's social media influencers are followers, likes, and shares, it's harder to determine whether they are providing real value, just popular or merely a pleasant distraction from the other things we really should be doing. And many of today's influencers are self-focused, self-aggrandizing, and self-congratulatory. "Look at me! Look at me!" seems to be the subliminal soundtrack running behind all that they produce.

As John Maxwell says, "Influence is leadership, and leadership is influence." So, by default, our influencers are our leaders. The key question then becomes "Where are your influencers leading you?"

In *Generous Influencers*, Robert Kaelin is talking about a very different kind of influence – influence that is focused on others. Influence that has a strong thread of humility and kindness running through it. Influence that is about serving and making the world a better place. Influence that is leadership at its best. Generous leadership.

If you can learn to lead that way, you'll build a legacy of positive impact that extends beyond yourself, your personal sphere of influence, and your lifetime.

I first met Robert Kaelin at a Maxwell Live2Lead event I co-hosted with my brother Mike Newman. When you meet Robert for the first time, you'll notice his infectious energy, enthusiasm, and warm personality. If you talk with him for more than a few minutes, you'll quickly see that his life and results show evidence of his commitment to his faith, genuine care for people, and life-long learning.

I've had the ongoing privilege of watching Robert pursue his dream of expanding his sphere of influence – not to make himself a big deal but to impact the lives of those around him in a positive way. He is doing this work both as a successful business owner and as a catalyst for growth in his business community. He also is the founder of the annual *Elevate!* Conference, where I've been honored to share the stage with him and other outstanding speakers as we work together to equip people and change lives. And now, Robert has condensed his experience and learning into this book, *Generous Influencers*.

If your goal is a million Instagram followers to tell you how awesome you are, or if the only reason you want to be a vice president or CEO is for the pay, the power, the perks, and the parking spot, then *Generous Influencers* is not for you. However, if you want to learn how to make a difference through generous leadership focused on helping and serving others, this book delivers!

Robert outlines what it means to be a Generous Influencer and shows real-world examples of what that looks like. Then he gives you practical steps and tools to become the kind of person who is bigger on the inside than you are on the outside, so you have the capacity to lead with generosity.

If that's what you want, I'm confident you'll enjoy this book as much I have. Buckle up and get ready! *Generous Influencers* will change your life and equip you to change the lives of others.

Karl J. Newman
Speaker, Author, and CEO

PREFACE

Growing up, I didn't know what was wrong, but I had a sense
that there was something better –something more to life.
Through junior high and high school, I felt this. When I
had my first child, it became stronger. When my wife and I got
married, life got more complex, but I still felt it. Then, I went to
college in my late twenties and, while I couldn't put my finger
on it then either, something happened that changed my life. For
years, I was on a journey to find out how I could be the best version of me I could possibly be for the world.

I believe I have found the answer that fills the gap: generosity. As a person of faith, I know there is so much more to
what God calls each of us to than going through the motions and
trying to be a good person. Ultimately, God's call requires us to
experience transformation and healing so we can begin to understand how we have been created and what our unique purpose is.

I spent far too many years trying to connect the dots without
much help from mentors and leaders in my life giving me the
help I needed to get to where I am today. Perhaps I am just a

slow learner, but I think the ability for us to share information is at a critical point. We assume everyone knows what we know or that they can find it on this fancy thing called the internet. We literally have access to information that would make us seem like geniuses, but for some reason many aren't leveraging what is at their fingertips.

Why? Because we need models in our life to learn from, not information—not lectures, not education—models. We need leaders who are showing us what it should look like. That is why I wrote this book: to give you insights and tools to help you find purpose, joy, abundance, and meaningful connections while creating positive impact by living generously. I want to share what I have learned and help you skip the years of mistakes, frustrations, and challenges that have allowed me to build great relationships and positively impact my community.

~Robert Kaelin

INTRODUCTION

If you have picked up this book, my guess is that you are intrigued by the idea of living generously. Perhaps you are in a place of either trying to understand what living generously looks like for yourself or to figure out how to add value to others by living a generous life. The goal of this book is to accomplish both of those goals with what we are going to learn together.

My desire is for you to be both challenged and encouraged. I want this book to add value to you and I want you to add value to others by using TACT^2 (Tact squared):

Thinking and considering what you are learning
Applying what you learn to your life
Changing what that needs to be changed
T^{2}eaching what you learn to others

After all, the concept of applying "TACT^2" fits right in line with living generously.

I have slowly learned through trial and error, failure and struggle, that there is nothing more important than relationships. Everything is about relationships: with God, yourself, and the world around you.

Think about the people you love most. Now imagine that you treated them poorly in some instance. Did this drive a wedge between you? Anytime we do something that drives a wedge between us and another, we are damaging our relationships. We are thinking about ourselves first. The reality is, at the end of the day, relationships are all we have. We have all experienced this to some degree—after all, none of us is perfect.

Admitting that to ourselves helps to reinforce the idea that nobody is perfect, even us. We have all made mistakes and we will make mistakes again. We can't be too hard on ourselves for making them. We need to learn from them and move forward. Start small. Choose to do one generous act.

The idea for this book came one day as I was developing a way to engage with people to influence the culture in the city where I live. I see a need for love, kindness, grace, leadership, and compassion—generosity—to be spread all over. For people to accept each other for who they are and be kind and plentiful, with grace and mercy, even when they disagree. But it kept coming back to, *What can I do but start right where I am?* If we want to see change, we must first lead it by our own example.

So, I started a group called Generous Influencers. The purpose of this group was three-fold:

1. to simply give people permission to be involved and to live generously

2. to help guide people down the path of personal growth
3. to give people a platform with guidance on how to do the first two things

I hope you find this book helpful and can take what I have been learning to new heights. I, in no way, aim to explore everything pertaining to living generously, but rather seek to touch on what I know and have experienced to give us a baseline to practice a lifestyle that transforms lives and communities.

It is my goal to keep the contents of this book simple to understand and easy to apply. I don't know about you, but I am a "book-writer-in-er" (and a word coiner as well). I invite you to do the same and underline, mark it up, add comments—whatever helps make the content memorable for you.

One thing I hope you will do, using the acronym TACT^2 I mentioned above, is to mark T in this book for the areas you need to think deeply on and consider. Perhaps you may even need to do some more research to develop and understand the concepts and ideas more fully. Then, an A for the things you need to apply, a C for the things you want to change, and a T^2 for what you need to teach to someone else. You see, when we grow and learn, it multiplies our impact to others. That's where the (^{2}) comes in; it reminds us that the Teaching T is where we get to leverage exponential impact of sharing what we learn with others.

Using this method will not only help you; it will multiply into the lives of others and impact them too. This method is particularly helpful when we are being intentional about our growth. I highly encourage you to use it as well.

I also encourage you to go through this book with another person or group, if you are able. There are discussion and personal reflection questions at the end of each chapter designed to be discussed and help you apply the material to your daily life. If you want to take it even deeper, there is additional content on my website (www.robertjkaelin.com).

I believe you have it inside you to make huge impact in the lives of those around you!

God bless you on this journey, my friend.

Chapter 1

THE PATH TO GENEROSITY

L iving generously is a lifestyle goal many see as a worthy aspiration in their lives. From philanthropic work to parenting, "generosity" means we are giving to others in meaningful and impactful ways. Generosity is the act of both being kind and plentiful to another with grace and mercy. We all can agree that generosity is virtuous, and it blesses both the giver and recipient. I love seeing generosity in action and how it unfolds. You never know just how an act of generosity might change someone's life!

In 2014, a large church organization was building a new campus in Louisville, Kentucky. About one month before the new church was set to open, pastor Dave Stone received a letter from the lead pastor of a church just a mile down the street. The letter read:

Dear Dave,

We are located less than five minutes from Southeast's new campus that you are currently building. It's common

*for churches to feel a sense of competition with each other,
for natural reasons, and we have even wrestled with some
of those same emotions since we heard you all are building
a campus near us. But we want you to know that we believe
in Southeast and what you are doing to reach this city for
Jesus Christ, and we are praying for you as you launch your
new campus.*

*We have included with this letter a financial gift for
your building fund. This is a sacrificial gift from our church
staff to let you know how much we believe in what you are
doing and to remind us that we are a family serving this city
together. If your treasure is where your heart is, we want our
heart to be for your success.*

We are praying and we are believing with you.
Pastor Jason Isaacs
Hope City Church

This letter was also signed by four or five other individuals
who made up the entirety of the Hope City Church staff. This
little church staff had given a check enclosed with the letter for
$1,000. Southeast Church, at the time, had a regular attendance
of 20,000 people. Hope City was seeing about 200 people per
week. Their generosity was not only unexpected; it was counter
to what we see in the world. Why does this story matter? Because
there is way more to generosity than meets the eye.

Hope City Church didn't give to Southeast Church
because they were swimming in money. They gave because
they believed in the purpose and mission—and it resulted in
living generously.

Giving is great! There is no doubt that giving makes us feel good. When we see someone else light up because of our generosity, it puts a smile on our face. Think about giving a birthday gift to someone you love. You have heard them talk about this thing for some time. You just know that they will love it! To watch them open the gift is almost like a gift for you too.

Generosity Starts with Wholeness

This type of giving—gifts and such—comes easily when we have the means to make it happen, but what happens when we are stretched thin? How do we overcome the challenge of living generously when we don't have the margins?

Exasperation!

This is the one word I would use to best describe how I saw my mother's experience during my childhood. I didn't know it then, but when I learned what that word meant, it was a lightbulb moment. I am not saying she did a bad job as a mom. In fact, she did quite a good job of navigating the challenges she had in front of her.

Mom's exasperation was a symptom of a bigger problem: she was running a burnout cycle, primarily out of a desire to give and serve, yet without the emotional and financial resources she desperately needed. As kids, we helplessly watched it happen again and again. Humans aren't designed to operate like batteries. We don't work best when depleted of energy and resources. We work best plugged into the outlet, when we are plugged into the source and things flow through us.

Growing up, my siblings and I watched her as she served us to her detriment. She worked a full-time job to come home and care for her three children. Cooking, cleaning, laundry, shopping, bills, and all the adulting that two parents struggle with doing on a regular basis, she did all by herself. She really did pour everything she had into others. The problem was, she pushed beyond her capacity, and in doing so, was indirectly teaching my siblings and me to live out unhealthy boundaries ourselves. Her cup would often run empty, and she would break down and need long periods of recovery. Can you imagine how draining this life must have been for her?

Perhaps you know someone who has had a similar experience. As for me, I began my early adult life in much the same way as my mom. After all, it was what I knew: not giving the best of me, but giving what was left of me. That is no way to live! There are many people living this way, giving away what they do not have to give. There is a problem with this kind of giving. It is not coming from a place of wholeness. If, on the other hand, we are giving from a place of wholeness, it will eliminate the burnout cycle in our lives. It will allow us to show up regularly and truly live generously.

The struggle with finding wholeness is that it is work. It is messy and hard. We offer excuses for why we can't do the hard, messy, work: we are *"busy,"* we are doing the best we can, and we are striving to keep up with all that is going on in the world. This keeps us from the hard work of wholeness that leads to burnout. Burnout is a gradual process and can be a tough cycle to get out of. It will steal your motivation and passion, and leave you feeling defeated, discouraged, and frustrated. This is why it is crucial that we do the good, hard work to avoid it!

Getting to Work on Getting Whole

The total personal debt in the US is $16.64 trillion[1]. The median household debt is $59,800. The median US household income is $59,039[2]. This is an alarming statistic considering that, if 100 percent of the median household income was to pay off debt for a year, it still wouldn't suffice. Considering this, it's clear that most of us have more going out than coming in. Most of us clearly have a problem with spending more than we have in the bank. This practice has impacted other aspects of our lives as well.

Think about your personal budget. If you have a set amount of income coming in every month, that is the amount you have to spend. If you exceed this amount, you find yourself going into debt by the amount you overspent. Doing this regularly will be taxing on you and your family and can have drastic consequences.

To operate a healthy household, we need to budget our income. When we keep track of our budget, we know exactly how much we can spend. We have a specified dollar amount that has been allocated for a specific expense or category. When we don't budget, we operate off what we expect there to be in the account. *Oops, I forgot about that auto withdrawal!* These little errors come with fees, and they stack up over time. The same is true for how we spend our time, and our ability to live generously.

Nobody wants the burden of debt hanging over them like a dark cloud. We shudder at the idea of bankruptcy and what that would mean for our lives, but we continue to find ourselves in the same financial predicaments.

The answer to this dilemma is *personal wholeness.* If you are giving and it is draining you, that is not generosity; that is a burden, like my mom experienced. Living with generosity in a healthy way can only come from a place of wholeness: mentally, physically, spiritually, and relationally.

Don't get me wrong, wholeness does not mean perfection. It means we are not operating from a place of scarcity. How much (mental, physical, spiritual, relational) equity do you have in the bank? How do you know how much you can give? Are you spending more than you have in the bank? Why is it that there seems to be such a large disconnect between the ways in which we desire to live (the ideal life) and the way in which we are currently living (current reality)? The answers to these questions can all be found in seeking wholeness first.

Living in Wholeness

I believe there are four primary areas that make up our whole selves: spiritual, mental, physical, and relational. These areas make up the wholeness of a person and when not complete, it creates brokenness in our lives. Let's take a look at all four of these:

1. Spiritual—What sets the standard for your life?

We are starting with spirituality because all things begin and end in the spiritual realm. Think about it: you have an idea (spiritual) before you can take action (physical). Once you take action, you have impact (spiritual). This is an important process to note because what we are after is truth. Being able to articulate things in the spiritual realm can be difficult, at times. Talking about spirituality brings about many preconceived notions and conscious biases one may have. The reality is we are spiritual beings. As writer C.S. Lewis aptly said, "You don't have a soul. You are a soul. You have a body."

For some, "spirituality" brings up ideas and experiences of God or religion, some of which may be good and positive, some of which may be unpleasant or confusing. While there are many expressions of this part of our humanity, we are all on a spiritual journey. On this journey, we are all looking for answers to the spiritual questions in this life. Our soul will not be satisfied until we find the answer. The truth. The way. Our worldview comes from the answers we find on this journey.

The way I am defining spirituality is this: *spirituality is one's inner submission to a higher power.* In this sense, we are giving authority to something of influence and allowing it to establish our path and guiding principles moving forward. In other words, we are operating in the "spirit" of said authority.

Spirituality is demonstrated by all, even those who may not even believe they are spiritual, by submitting to things that control us: fear, comfort, medication, status, power, intelligence, alcohol, escapism, and the list goes on. When we submit to comfort, for example, we operate in the spirit of said thing. Our choices are made to not compromise this highest authority in our lives. Allowing comfort to be the authority, we may choose not to take a chance on something because we are fearful of stepping out of our comfort zone. Is that healthy? Is that what is best? Spiritual health is derived from giving oneself over to a higher power that not only adds value but does so in a way that does not compromise truth or wholeness in any way. Some call this a moral compass. This is where wholeness begins and should always be the first place of personal reflection and examination if brokenness is presented.

As a person of faith, my relationship with God sets the path upon which my steps are taken. The teachings of Jesus, and the example he sets in the Bible, give me my moral compass with which to operate in my life. I encourage you to ask yourself: what has the ultimate authority, that moral compass, in *your* life? I would take it a step further and ask, is that compass serving you to become whole or is it keeping you from wholeness?

Sometimes the things that serve as our compass don't actually point us north. When a compass is off, it leads us in the wrong direction. Imagine being in the forest and all you have is a compass. Here's what you know. You have enough food and water for three days. There is help 60 miles away, you'll need to cover 20 miles a day, and your help is a small cabin in the middle of the forest with everything you need. But what you don't know is that your compass is off by one degree. As you set off, you assume the compass is right. When you arrive at your destination, you are over a mile away from the help you desperately need, with no bearings for how to get there. Now imagine you have others with you who rely on your leadership to get them to where they need to go. Wouldn't you do everything before you set out to ensure your compass was pointing true north?

I know for me, I have been askew from true north and it has hurt others. When this happens, forgiveness becomes key: forgiveness of yourself to get back on the path and forgiveness of others whom you have hurt. Forgiveness plays a big role in all our lives. When present, it helps us to become whole. When absent, it damages our spiritual life, relational network, mental health, and physical well-being by harboring resentment and anger. You know the saying: "Hurt people hurt people." It's true!

Let me show you an example of what this has looked like in my own life. My wife and I got into a small tiff a while back. I had said something to which she took offense to and she began to give me the cold shoulder, and then I responded with the same in return. It was stupid and petty over something so small, when we could have just acknowledged the hurt, said apologies, and moved on. Quality time and physical touch being my love language, she may as well have just verbally told me she didn't love me anymore. Asking, "Why are you so upset?" wasn't helpful. This went on for two days. I was frustrated and hurt. She was frustrated and hurt.

She got up on Friday morning and got ready for work, but she got a bit more dressed up than normal. I didn't think anything of it at the time, but I did notice. I knew she was hanging out at a local event after work. As she walked out the door she said, "I'll be home later." Knowing that she was going to a specific event in town, I knew that the event was over at 9:00 p.m., I assumed she would hang out for about 30 minutes afterward to chit chat and would be home around 10:00 p.m. . . . but 11:30 p.m. rolled around and I still hadn't heard from her. Did she get into an accident? Did something bad happen to her? My mind raced and adrenaline began pumping through my system.

I reached for my phone on my nightstand and checked the *Find My iPhone* app. She was at a bar in a neighboring big city. Was she cheating on me? (Unbelievably, that was the first thought that raced through my mind.) The initial reaction was deep hurt and anger. I had to wrestle the emotions I was feeling and accept that she was choosing to do that. I couldn't believe it. (From something so stupid, my world was changing in an instant.)

When my wife got home, I was packed and leaving to stay somewhere else. We didn't talk.

I went to church on Sunday. She was there too. We sat next to each other and pretended that everything was okay, that we weren't hurting. Inside, the story was different. There was so much distance between us. I thought I knew this person. The trust we had built over the years was deep and connected. From something so small, in such a short time, we had become like distant hostile enemy countries: each pursuing the best for ourselves and not each other anymore.

After church, we were drawn into a short conversation, which, thankfully, turned into hours. She explained the circumstances of the previous evening and how things had played out. I told her my side of the story and how hurt I was that she would do that.

She had gone out with a girlfriend to the planned event and was invited afterwards to hear her friend sing karaoke. She wasn't cheating on me, like I had played out in my mind. (Such a ridiculous assumption!) But while I was certainly relieved, I was still wrestling with forgiving her because of the lack of communication and how it had caused me to panic and draw the worst possible conclusions.

She admitted she was wrong and I admitted I was wrong. We forgave each other and vowed to learn from this situation and not allow it to be repeated in our lives. I attribute our ability to forgive and overcome this bump in our relationship to our spiritual and moral compass, and the role God plays in our marriage.

The interesting thing is, if we hadn't been previously arguing, she would have communicated her plan and I would have said, "Sounds like fun! Be safe. I'll see you when you get home." And all of it would have been avoided. However, we wouldn't have had the opportunity to generously forgive each other for the hurts and learn from our mistakes.

A lack of forgiveness (bitterness) is often what hinders us from spiritual health. When bitterness resides inside our heart, it expresses itself in a variety of ways—mentally, physically and relationally. After all, hurt people hurt people. Learning to accept forgiveness for ourselves and to generously give it to others is key to maintaining a healthy spiritual life. Sometimes we need to forgive others, sometimes we need to forgive ourselves, and sometimes we need both.

2. Mental—What do you tell yourself?

We are the sum of our thoughts. Our mental health has to do with thinking true and good thoughts toward ourselves and others. Truthfulness doesn't allow for assumptions; something can only be true or not. This principle forces us to ask questions, and goodness keeps our thinking focused in a positive direction. Sadly, assumption and negativity plague us as humans. If we could ask more questions and encourage more often, the world would be a vastly different place.

Studies say we have as many as 60,000 thoughts per day. Of those, 80 percent are negative; 95 percent of those negative thoughts are reoccurring.[3] Think about that! If we are the sum of our thoughts, then it is no wonder we have a mental health crisis in our world. Our life is made up of our thoughts, most of which tend to be negative!

Think about it: have you ever had a thought and said to yourself, *That's too . . . (scary, hard, crazy, etc.)*? That's a negative thought, and you just talked yourself out of that effort. We do this all the time! This is us becoming the sum of our thoughts. What you tell yourself matters, what you allow others to tell you matters, and what you tell others matters.

When we feel like something is too hard (scary, crazy, etc.), it's important for us to recognize that emotion (fear) in our thoughts. Our emotions play a big part in how our thoughts are framed, and, though emotions feel very *real*, they aren't always *true*." Emotions are designed to function like a thermometer, not a thermostat. A thermostat controls the temperature of the room while a thermometer can only tell you what the temperature is. Emotions tell us what we are feeling, but it's up to us to ask why.

One of the most difficult decisions I have had to make was to go from working a corporate job to living as an entrepreneur: creating my own income, providing for my family, leaning on my skills and talents, and making it work on my own. The mental anguish was excruciating. *How will I make it work? What if I fail? What if I don't have what it takes? What if I don't know what I am doing?* What if this and what if that.

But what if it works? What if I don't fail?

The mental games we play in our heads make tough decisions even tougher. What I have found to work well is to have thought partners. When we share and process with people we trust, it helps us to get out of our own head. These are people who know you and understand you. People who listen and help you through these challenging situations. They remind us to ask why we are feeling or thinking a certain way.

When we ask ourselves why, we begin to evaluate and develop a response. Since many of our feelings come from a place of assumptions and negative thoughts, it is crucial, for the sake of our mental health, that we develop emotional intelligence and healthy coping mechanisms that will serve us and others.

We must break through the mental barriers that hold us back and keep us from living in a way in which we all desire to live. We are the sum of our thoughts and our wholeness hinges on our ability to effectively master our thoughts and manage our emotions.

3. Physical—How do you treat yourself?

There is more to our physical health than just diet and exercise; there are environmental factors like our home, communities, and work. There are experiential factors that contribute to our values systems and help develop our neural pathways. And there are genetic factors that play into our overall physical health as well.

However, of all the components to our physical health, we really only have control of the environmental and personal elements. The most important piece of the puzzle to our physical health is our personal choices when it comes to diet, exercise, and care. We can alter many things in this arena: what we eat (how much and how often), how we exercise (and how regularly), where we live, what we do for work, and even whom we hang around. With all this in mind, our physical health can often be a secondary priority.

Our bodies are incredible! They are powerful, resilient, and a true marvel. The scientific community tells us our gut is like a second brain. When it comes to our diet, we have all heard "you are what you eat" and I believe that is true. The nutrients we pour into our bodies contribute to the output we get from them. Eating fast food all the time leaves us lacking proper nutrients and feeling sluggish and depleted of energy. On the contrary, a balanced diet can renew us and give us energy to do amazing things.

Regular exercise helps our bodies maintain a hormonal balance that lifts our mental health and improves many systems like the cardiovascular, muscular, and pulmonary systems, as well as being linked to improving sleep, and memory, while combatting a plethora of conditions and diseases.

My mother-in-law shared a story with me of a time when she sent a pig to the butcher. They dropped off their pig and came back a couple days later to pick up the meat. She said they could tell they'd picked up someone else's pig because it smelled like mint. The butcher had accidentally switched meat between her and another customer. The problem was, the pig she received had pillaged a field of mint leaves and not only smelled like mint, but it tasted like mint. Just like this pig, we become what we eat—or maybe a better way to say it is the food we consume makes us what we are.

When we are not physically active; the last thing we feel motivated to do is exercise. Motivation does not come first. Determination does. We have to make the choice to take control of our situations and form new healthier habits. Treating yourself compassionately with proper diet, exercise, and care will serve you well in the long run. Our wholeness depends on our ability to discipline ourselves to care for our physical bodies.

4. Relational—How do you add to yourself and others?

Healthy relationships are essential to our overall well-being. As we all experience, understanding and sustaining relationships are difficult at best, like the experience Jackie and I had with her night out that was supposed to be fun. Why is that?

The easy answer is relationships are complex and require us to think deeply. Successful relationships ultimately require two or more people to agree on a set of responsibilities while operating in a set of boundaries within the reality of varying personalities, abilities, goals, perspectives, and motivations. All the while, those factors, more often than not, are never discussed between the two parties, which frequently leads to unspoken (and therefore unmet) expectations, a common source of conflict in relationships.

Let's consider first our relationship with the spiritual authority in our life. What is yours? How does it impact your life? How does it cause you to impact the lives of those around you? This primary foundation is the foundation on which the rest of your life is built.

Second is the relationship with yourself. The more we understand ourselves, the more we understand and appreciate others. The relationships you have with others will be the outcome of those first two relationships.

The truth still stands that, as humans, we need relationships. We are social creatures and are limited in our ability to be completely self-sufficient. We need things from others and each person has something unique they bring to their relationships, whether in skill, personality, talent, experience, and/or perspective. Living in community with others requires us to lean on each other for these things.

And, even more than transactional needs, we need love from others. We need guidance, mentorship, and encouragement—we need others to help us become the best versions of ourselves. Relationships help to round off our sharp edges and balance our thinking as we process the various aspects of life.

My wife and I have been together for 16 years, at the time of writing this book. We have had our share of ups, downs, sideways, crossways, long ways, short ways, big ways, small ways, and everywhere in between, but the thing that keeps us going is our commitments to God and each other. She sure knows I am not perfect and I know the same of her. We can't expect that of each other, yet often we choose to hold others to a higher standard than we operate in ourselves. When I fail, I give myself excuses because I know I was trying my best and that my intentions were good. When she fails, I need to offer that same grace to her. Do I? Not always, but it has been a focus as I work through and live out the concept of treating others how I want to be treated.

This area of focus can be harder or easier depending on how you are wired, which we will talk about later. However, it's important we realize how critical relational health is to our wholeness and our ability to live generously in community with others.

The Balance of Wholeness

When it comes to balancing mental, physical, spiritual, and relational health, we must first be aware that this balance is not the status quo in our culture, it is the exception. Wholeness should be the status quo because it is essential to happiness, health, and overall well-being.

When we look at how the World Health Organization defines complete health, it's no wonder the world struggles with wholeness: "A state of complete physical, mental, and social well-being and not merely the absence of disease or infirmity."[4] This definition is missing the spiritual aspect! This is actually the most important aspect of wholeness because it is the beginning.

For me, Jesus, is the center and circumference of all things in my life. For you, it is whatever spiritual authority you submit to. Out of the spiritual is where the health, or lack thereof, in the other areas stem from. All four areas are connected. They exist in a relationship to each other. The healthiness in one area has an impact on the health of the others. When one of the four parts is left out, it makes it impossible to establish wholeness.

As we navigate the path wholeness (and eventually to abundance and generosity), we will inevitably continue to experience issues and seasons of life in which our constant striving for wholeness will always be present. These categories we just looked at (mental, physical, spiritual, relational) can help us evaluate and check our state of overall health in the various seasons we find ourselves in. The most important thing to consider here is that they all contribute to the overall health of each other. Therefore, best practice is to evaluate and consider them on a regular basis.

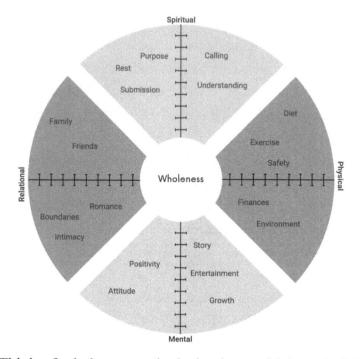

Think of wholeness as the bedrock on which we build our house. As we aim for wholeness, we are excavating the ground and establishing a firm foundation on which the rest of our lives is built. Wholeness gives us healing, balance, and overall health in these areas of our lives and allows us to enter a new paradigm of living generously. When we understand that, and balance these areas well, we can value and love ourselves and others through generosity.

Questions for Reflection and Discussion

This section of each chapter is to help you think through what you have just read and apply it to your life. As you reflect on what you just read:

1. What stood out to you in this last chapter?

2. In what ways did you use TACT[2] in this last chapter? How will you follow up with those notes?

3. Which aspect(s) of wholeness (mental, physical, spiritual, relational) do you need to dedicate some attention to? What will you do to address each area?

4. As you look at the wholeness diagram, rate yourself from 1-10 in the following areas.

   a. How would you rate yourself in Spiritual wholeness?

   b. How would you rate yourself in Physical wholeness?

   c. How would you rate yourself in Mental wholeness?

   d. How would you rate yourself in Relational wholeness?

5. Based on your ratings in the previous questions, what would your overall wholeness rating be?

6. If you were to put effort in to balance your life, what boundaries do you need to set up or remove? How will this help you move forward?

7. What do you need to do to ensure that you continue operating from a place of wholeness moving forward?

Chapter 2

VALUING SELF, VALUING OTHERS— THE FOUNDATION OF GENEROSITY

O nce you have a substantial degree of wholeness, caring for yourself well, you are on the way to being able to love and value others from a place of abundance, instead of scarcity. That is when we can truly add value to others.

Imagine you have three empty cups on the counter in front of you. You take the first cup, place it under the faucet, and let the water trickle into it. Eventually, that cup will begin to overflow. The water that begins to overflow from the cup, that is the *abundance*. Abundance is like the water that overflows from the cup. This abundance becomes the margin we have to give to others. Because we are overflowing, we can give.

Now imagine the second cup has a small hole in it; the water is still pouring in at a trickle, but the water going in is flowing faster than the water leaving the cup from the tiny hole. The cup can still overflow and has margin for generosity.

Finally, imagine the third cup. This cup has a hole in it as well, but this hole isn't so tiny. Let's imagine the hole is the size of the base of the cup. Water, no matter how fast it flows, will never fill that cup. Therefore, it will never overflow.

We must value ourselves enough to care for the holes and cracks in our cup so we can value others out of the margin we create from overflowing. If we want to live a life of generosity, it begins with valuing ourselves and then overflows into others. Valuing others is the foundation upon which our house is built. While valuing others is the foundational principle for living a generous life, it is only sustainable if we are living in wholeness and able to value ourselves first.

Abundance and Overflow

Living generously is the capacity to be kind and, from our abundance, overflow into others. Generosity by nature has nothing to do with what the giver gets in exchange and everything to do with adding value to the other person on the receiving end. It also has nothing to do with how much is given. In fact, sometimes the smallest gestures can be the most generous. Since generosity is giving from overflow, it is dependent on the overflow in the life of the giver.

I observed this principle when my wife and I started gardening in our back yard. We would plant all sorts of things. It was an exciting and great learning experience for the whole family. We loved the times when we would just go into the garden and pull weeds. It didn't require our brain power to do it. It was tedious work that allowed us time to reflect, think, and pray.

Being amateur backyard "farmers" meant we got to grow food for our family. Every day, we would do something to tend to the garden. The biggest challenge for me was always right after we planted. Often, I wanted to dig in the dirt to see if the seeds were growing yet. I had to learn patience, sure, but I also had to learn to value the process. As with anything that grows, there is always a process to that growth. If we do not value and respect the process, we can compromise the growth altogether and create bigger problems for ourselves and others down the road. That can point us right back to our personal growth.

We must value the process; accepting that we are all on a journey gives us room to wrestle with our thoughts, ideas, experiences, and put the outcomes into practice. This rhythm of trial and error is what we call *life*. As we grow, we take these lessons with us and have a choice to share them with others or to keep them to ourselves.

Trust the process. There are things happening under the soil.

There is an interesting dichotomy to valuing others. That is, you can't do it until you first value yourself. You must see your value before you begin to add value to others. John Maxwell calls this the "Law of the Mirror" in his book *The 15 Invaluable Laws for Growth.*

Relationships are hard. Everyone has needs, wants, desires, and plans, while at the same time we are all in different places in our journey. There are many things that get in the way of valuing others. The biggest one is selfishness. We tend to not like that word. We can spot it with eagle eyes in others, but when it comes to ourselves, we walk around with blinders on.

We tend to be in our own way, and this isn't easy to overcome.

(Un)Limited Generosity

Over time, words often inherit new meanings in the hearts and minds of the people who use them. Dictionaries were invented to keep us on the same page when it comes to language. However, even with the advent of dictionaries, we still find that meanings can shift over time. With the concept of generosity, there is a tendency for us to think about it in terms of financial giving; however, generosity comes in many forms, doesn't it? The definition of being kind and overflowing shouldn't be limited to being kind and overflowing with *money*, right?

We know people can be generous with their time, talents, kindness, encouragement, positivity, creativity, service, compassion, listening, knowledge, and more. I am sure there are many other examples you can think of that are not included in that list. But money generally floods our minds when we think of generosity.

The name of the city where I grew up is called Puyallup (pronounced Pew–ALL-up), in Washington State. The history of this city, which was incorporated in 1890, is fascinating. The name originated from the Puyallup Tribe of Native Americans and means "generous and welcoming behavior to all people (friends and strangers) who enter our lands." Over the last 120 years, the meaning of Puyallup has been pushed into the shadows and many residents have never even heard of it. However, language builds culture and Puyallup over the last several years has had leaders who are reminding the people to remember their roots.

This is just one example of how words can be limited by our understanding of them, and it takes others to help us see the true meaning behind the word. Parents, teachers, friends, and leaders alike can influence and encourage us to embrace the positive impact of generosity in its fullness. That is what we are on a path to discovering here.

There are four practices we can build onto our foundation of valuing others that will help us walk out generosity in our lives. These become the walls, doors, windows which make up the house we invite others into. These practices include:

Practice 1—Abundance

Abundance is the result of the foundation being established. Going with the cup illustration, abundance is the overflow by which we can give without emptying the cup of ourselves. It is the excess, the surplus, the extra we can offer without taking away from our own need. There's nothing we need to do besides ensure how we are using the resources given to us.

I heard a great question once: *Are we living as a reservoir or a river?*

Reservoirs hold water and retain it; think of an artificial lake. If it empties, it does not fill back up. It simply becomes a large crater in the ground. A giant grave. While rivers flow from the source to the ocean, they are always flowing *through*. Depending on the season, they can be raging or docile. A river does not hold any of itself back. It isn't worried about not having enough water. It is simply a conduit to get water from the source to its destination.

The same is true for generosity. We can either hold onto it and keep it to ourselves or we can let it flow through us and into others. I don't know about you, but I want to be a river, flowing into others and filling their cup so they can do the same in the lives of others.

Operating in a mindset of abundance allows us to recognize that there is always plenty for us. We don't have to worry about not having enough.

Are you a river or a reservoir?

Practice 2–Sacrifice

Something is only worth what someone else is willing to pay for it. In other words, the person has value in your eyes and is worthy of your generosity: time, talent, treasure, etc.

There has never been an act of generosity that didn't cost the giver something. Since we can always be doing something else, time generously spent with someone is a sacrifice made that could have been spent elsewhere. Gifts generously given include thought, time, and money. Words generously spoken are also thought, time, and energy that could have been put toward something else. Generosity is always sacrificial in some way based on the value you can bring to the other person.

We have all sat under the shade of a tree we didn't plant.

Several months ago, Pastor Dave, whom I introduced in Chapter 1, was in Arizona when he received a text from a friend in Kentucky, which said, "I have some money I would like for you to give away to the ministry of your choice." It was a substantial amount. Dave had never seen so many zeros. As a pastor, he began to think of all the ministries that could benefit from a portion of this gift. He replied and asked if he could disperse the funds between several ministries. The giver agreed.

On his trip back to Kentucky, on the final leg of his trip, he was thinking and praying about the list of ministries to which he would disperse the funds and how much each would receive. When they landed, Dave stood up to grab his luggage from the overhead compartment. As he was pulling down the bag, a gentleman spoke up from about three rows back.

"Hey Dave! I just wanted you to know that we appreciate everything you and your church do for the community."

"Thanks, man. That means a lot." replied Dave.

Feeling the pressure of everyone behind him needing to get their bags, he made his way off the plane and waited for his new friend to meet him in the terminal. When the man appeared, Dave began to walk and talk with him as they made their way to the baggage claim.

As they journeyed together through the concourse, Dave found out that the man was also a pastor in town.

"What is your name?" Dave asked.

"Jason Isaacs," he said.

It just so happened that this man was the same Jason Isaacs who, years earlier, had given Dave's church $1,000 for the building fund. They had talked on the phone but had never met in person until now.

"You'll never know how much that encouraged us. What a display of obedience to what God put on your heart," Dave proclaimed.

It was at that moment that Dave knew exactly where some of that money was going to go. He invited Jason to a lunch meeting a few weeks later, where they continued their conversation from the airport. Dave had prepared a letter for Jason that he gave him after the meal:

Jason,

The gift you and your church gave us seven years ago was a huge encouragement. I've always wanted your act of generosity to be multiplied. Now, because of a friend's obedience to God's prompting, and this friend's sacrifice and generosity, Hope City Church can be blessed.

"Then Peter spoke up, 'We have left everything to follow you!' 'Truly I tell you,' Jesus replied, 'no one who has left home or brothers or sisters or mother or father or children or fields for me and the gospel will fail to receive a hundred times as much in this present age: homes, brothers, sisters, mothers, children and fields—along with persecutions—and in the age to come eternal life.'" Mark 10:28-30

Sincerely,

Dave Stone

Then, Dave asked one final question of Jason: "Do you remember how much you gave?"

Without missing a beat, Jason replied, "A thousand dollars."

Dave reached his hand across the table and handed Jason a folded check worth $100,000. One hundred times the initial investment. Jason wept for a solid minute and then thanked him and revealed that over the past few weeks he had become quite discouraged as doors had been closing left and right and he was questioning whether he was supposed to stop trying to grow his church or not.

At that moment, generosity changed the world. Both men were impacted by the generosity of each other's actions, and the actions of others.

Again, how many of us have sat under the shade of a tree we didn't plant?

The reality is that we always have a choice. When we recognize the intentional sacrifice of generosity, we can start to appreciate the act a bit more as a receiver.

The beauty of sacrifice and generosity is that there is always a return on investment: better relationships, deeper connections, lives changed, people loved, or a project impacted.

Sacrificing for someone isn't a burden when it is focused on others. If it becomes a burden, we have not been giving out of abundance, but rather a place of emptiness. Or we may have some impure motive. When we sacrifice for people and feel burdened by it, we need to stop and go back to the source and allow our cup to fill back up.

Practice 3—Communication

> "People may hear your words, but they feel your attitude." - John C. Maxwell

Effective communication is a practice of generosity. It speaks volumes that someone would take the time and effort to ensure two parties are clear and on the same page. Unclear or unspoken expectations are investments into future resentment. Effective communication also allows us to connect tangible needs with tangible acts generosity.

Studies have shown that words account for seven (7) percent of the meaning of what is communicated, tone is 38 percent, and body language makes up the remaining 55 percent. When I use the word "communication," this is what

I am talking about. It's true: our actions speak louder than our words.

We need to learn to communicate so others know what we are really trying to convey: *You matter, I notice you, I love you, I want to help you, I am for you, etc.* Remember, that comes from our body language, tone, and words.

Once, a traveling salesman came to my door to sell a vacuum. I mentioned up front that we weren't interested, but he insisted. After multiple rejections, he finally said, "Oh, just let me show you what it can do and you may change your mind. It won't take long." Reluctantly, I let him in to show me how it worked and to deliver his pitch that he had worked on. Thirty minutes later, when he finished, my wife reminded him that we weren't interested, and he became aggressive with his sales tactics. Frankly, it was a little scary. He began shouting and aggressively putting his gear away. He muttered things like, "Make me load all this in here, for what?!" Clearly, his motive was not to benefit us in any way with his company's product. His motive was to make a sale.

Now, who knows his situation? He may not have had a sale in a while and was becoming desperate to feed his family, but the point is that his motive was very clear. Some cases aren't this obvious, but motives are always brought out into the light at some point.

Have you ever experienced someone say something with an ulterior motive? It can be very easy at times to feel the ulterior motives of others. Maybe you have had a similar experience in your life. For me, this man's actions spoke way louder than his words. And to boot, there was NEVER EVER any way after this that he would get any of my business.

When we communicate with people, we need to move out of our own way in order to connect with them. The salesman could have said something like, "Oh, you're not interested, okay. Here's my card. If you ever need anything or if you change your mind, it has our website on it and you can check out some of the videos there that show you the unique features of our machines. Have a great day!"

Instead, he got in his own way with the need to make a sale.

In John Maxwell's book, *Everyone Communicates, Few Connect,* he states, "Connecting is never about me. It's about the person with whom I'm communicating. Similarly, when you are trying to connect with people, it's not about you—it's about them. If you want to connect with others, you must get over yourself."[5]

Listening is not simply hearing. Listening is all about understanding. Not only are we hearing the words, but we are also hearing the attitude, motives, and idiosyncrasies of the other person.

I recently did a livestream where the audio was terrible. I had planned out some questions to ask in this interview and had prepared well for the interview, but the audio was so hard for me to hear that I had trouble connecting with the person on the other end. I was interrupting in the middle of sentences and changing the subject when I could have asked another meaningful question. It was embarrassing, but a valuable lesson in the importance of connection.

Connection is key. You need to be able to listen to communicate.

Active listening helps us to understand even better. It allows us to ask meaningful questions in the exchange of information and communicates that we care about the person who is talking. We are not just waiting for our turn to say what we were thinking while they were talking. This is an art and takes practice.

Remember earlier when I said effective communication also allows us to connect tangible needs with tangible acts of generosity? My friend Johnathan Waller and I were having a conversation over a cup of coffee when he shared the idea that we need to communicate our needs to give the opportunity for someone else to be generous. If people don't know you have a need, how can they act generously? By not sharing a need, we are ultimately denying a generous act the opportunity to even exist.

Because life is about relationship, communication is one of the most important things we can learn. It also helps us to move into our next area of practice.

Practice 4—Service

The Rotary Club has a saying, "Service above self." As we learn about ourselves, it makes it easier to serve. What we know about generosity is that it is based on valuing others and exhibited by our commitment to be kind and giving to others.

As I mentioned before, we cannot add value to others until we know our own value.

Jesus once said it this way, "Why do you look at the speck of sawdust in your brother's eye and pay no attention to the plank in your own eye? How can you say to your brother, 'Let me take the speck out of your eye,' when all the time there is a plank in your own eye? You hypocrite, first take the plank out of your own eye, and then you will see clearly to remove the speck from your brother's eye."[6]

Once we can see clearly, we can begin to serve others with clarity. We can see the root of the human condition and what is needed to help someone take the next step in their journey.

Blessing others through service is intentionally creating an opportunity for relationship with them. Service is one way we can show others that they matter, that they have value, that they have something to offer this world too.

We serve this way out of love. Dr. Tony Evans defines love in his book *Kingdom Family* as "compassionately and righteously pursuing the well-being of another."[7] There are two things here that focus on serving: the act of pursuit and the intent of that pursuit being for the well-being of another. Pursuit is an action word that means to chase after or to take interest in. When we chase after the well-being of another, that is love.

Serving others doesn't mean waiting on them hand and foot. While it can mean that—take hospitality, for example—what we are talking about is bigger and more important than just hospitality. We are anticipating opportunities to meet people's needs before they know that they need them.

For example, I have a real struggle with dishes. I am a soaker; getting them from the sink to the dishwasher as quickly as my wife would like is a challenge for me. I suppose, in my mind, I am always anticipating getting back to it later and making it easier on myself. However, for my wife, coming home to dishes makes her stressed. Knowing this, I can pursue her well-being by writing myself a note to put the dishes in the dishwasher or have the kids help me. It is a small thing, but it means a lot to her and shows her that I love her.

The Entrance

Building on the foundation of valuing others allows us to develop an abundance mindset, moving us with compassion to sacrifice for them, communicate with them, and serve with anticipation. These four practices become the walls, doors, windows which make up the house we invite others into. The walls stand tall on the foundation of valuing others. The windows allow people a peek inside. And the doors allow us to invite people into the beautiful home we are creating. When we invite people into our homes, we have established a new framework in our relationship. They are no longer outsiders; they are insiders. This is one of the richest blessings we can offer because it communicates to them that they belong. That they matter. When they come in, they will begin to see that generosity is the ultimate quality of a good leader.

Questions for Reflection and Discussion

This section of each chapter is to help you think through what you have just read and apply it to your life. As you reflect on what you just read:

1.   In what ways did you use TACT[2] in this last chapter? How will you follow up with those notes?

2.   In what ways have you received generosity from others in your life?

     a.   How does this show that they value you?

     b.   How do you value others currently? Be specific.

3.   How are you practicing these in your life: abundance, sacrifice, communication, and service?

4.   How can you continue to show value to others by your actions? Give an example.

5.   What is holding you back from living generously (or more generously)? Why do you believe that is holding you back?

6.   What appeals to you about living generously?

7.   What do you feel compelled to do after reading this chapter?

Chapter 3

GENEROSITY IN YOUR LIFE

W e bought a bright green neon light that says "Generous People" and hung it up in our café downtown to promote the idea of generosity in our city. People really love it! Over the past few years, this light has become a highlight for Elements' guests—and the selfie station in Puyallup was born. We love how it resonates with people and brings out the best in them.

One day, as I was behind the counter, a regular customer came up and asked me about it. As I shared the story and my belief about being generous, I could see his face light up.

"Let's grab coffee soon," he said, as he handed me his card.

When we connected a few weeks later, Neil shared his story with me. He had been running a non-profit organization called First Pursuit, which he had founded in 2004. He would get a group of guys to meet at the YMCA to play sports and build relationships with each other. Over the years, he impacted countless men. With many of them, the relationships that were forged con-

41

tinued to grow deeper over the years.

Since Neil had a non-profit, he would solicit donations to help fund these outings. It was simple, but that's all it had to be. He volunteered many hours in his life to create positive impact by pursuing the well-being of the men with whom he played sports. These men have carried the flag set by Neil, continuing the impact on others. They saw the example Neil set and used that as a model.

I loved hearing about all the impact Neil was making, under the radar, simply because he felt called to do so. He took something he loved and coupled it with purpose to make a difference in his community.

After asking me a dozen or so questions, Neil asked me if I would want to take over this work. I was taken back a bit because I wasn't expecting that. Many thoughts raced through my mind. I didn't know what to say.

I do know that my purpose in life is to add value to people and help them show up authentically, lead responsibly, and live generously. My gifts are encouragement, leadership, and vision.

So, how could I say no to an opportunity to take a purpose like that to the next level? The reality was, "I" couldn't.

Over the next bit of time, my team and I took that organization, rebranded it, and rebuilt it into what is now known as "Generous Influencers," an organization that aims to influence by living generously and leading in our community, while empowering, equipping, and encouraging others to do the same. Through this effort, we find it imperative to be and build the culture in our city that we want to see by making positive impact in the lives of those in our city. We do this through special events, leadership development, community building, and content creation, to name a few of our activities.

Our ultimate objective? To think and live generously, and make a positive impact in our community as a result.

Generosity Is an Opportunity

Generosity is an opportunity, but it is up to each of us to choose to act on it. When I was asked to take on the non-profit for Neil, the generous opportunity was presented to me. I had to choose how I would act. Then I had to choose how I was going to act within the organization to offer value back to the community.

The actions you take are based on what you believe about the world, yourself, and others. The foundation and principles we discussed in the last chapter help us to wrap our minds around generosity as a larger concept than just money. There are three areas in our life where we express generosity and have the most impact in the lives of others as a son, daughter, parent, friend, employee, co-worker, employer, or spouse. These are **Character**, **Calling**, and **Competency**.

Author Malcolm Webber penned, "Just as a stool has three legs, there are three foundations of effective leadership. All three must be *present* and in *balance* for the leader to succeed."

We should examine a few thoughts that will build on the last chapter and help us understand this principle more thoroughly. Then, let's sum up those thoughts with these questions: *Where are you going? How will you get there? How are you gifted?* These are leadership questions—self-leadership questions, specifically. These answers are complex and can take time to thoroughly work through. My encouragement to you is to sit with these for a while and think about them often.

As we grow and develop, we are regularly struck with some common pitfalls that can prevent us from realizing the full potential: *If I am called to it, it will just happen. I don't know how. I don't feel ready. I don't have the plan finalized. What if I look stupid? It's too hard. I don't want to screw it up.* These are all legitimate things that get in the way of us fully taking advantage of an opportunity. I am confident that as we begin to shift how we approach opportunities, that's when things change.

Opportunities present a natural problem, in that when they are presented, we aren't always able to seize them. In fact, I would argue that this is the case a majority of the time, and is what separates most people from true success. As Coach John Wooden famously said, "When opportunity knocks, it's too late to prepare."

This truth presses upon us the importance of the rest of this chapter, which is about doing the hard work to get you ready for the opportunities that living generously presents.

Calling: Where Are You Going?

Without a vision, the Bible says, people perish.[8] When we operate without vision, the dream—the goal, the project—eventually dies. People who once followed for one reason or another begin to fall off and find new things to occupy their precious time. The challenges of the original plan have become more costly to those involved than they are willing to put in. That's why having a clear vision has a dramatic effect on our ability to lead. When we lead with our vision in front, it brings the right people who care deeply and want to be part of it, and keeps them committed and engaged.

"Why is vision so important to calling," you say? Well, I'm glad you asked. Everything that has been designed has a purpose. A sign displayed on a building to get your attention and reveal the physical location of an organization. A bee that pollenates. A car that drives from point A to point B. And you. Your vision, your purpose, your why, your calling. No matter what you call it, you have a distinct purpose in your life. Because you are unique and there is no one else like you, you have a purpose in your life that no one else can fulfill. If you don't do it, who will? Who can?

> "The two greatest days are the day you were born and the day you figured out why." - Mark Twain

As I mentioned in the last chapter, the inability to seize opportunities is what separates most people from true success. What I mean by that statement is this: **You have an infinite amount of potential inside you; however, much of that potential has not been fully realized yet.**

Many of us do not have a clear understanding of what we were made for. Our uniqueness, as Rory Vaden puts it, hasn't been discovered yet. Simon Sinek calls this your "why," and wrote a terrific book aptly named *Starting with Why,* where he says, "Knowing WHY is not the only way to be successful, but it is the only way to maintain a lasting success and have a greater blend of innovation and flexibility." He uses a golden circle to illustrate that our why is the center of everything, and the place from which our HOW and WHAT come from. I highly recommend working through Simon Senek's book; while geared toward business, the principles can translate to your personal life.

As a child, I dreamt of being a supercross racer and flying through the air as I cleared a 90-foot triple with camera flashes going off in the stadium around me. Later, I found myself excited about the idea of touring the world as a famous musician. However, I didn't pursue either of those activities—not because I stopped loving them, but ultimately because I wasn't called to them. I eventually gave up those dreams in search for something more fulfilling and life giving. If certain dreams don't stick with you, it doesn't mean you don't enjoy them, but it does mean they aren't your calling.

Many times, we can find what we are called to do, our why, by looking back. As we grow and align with our values and giftings, clarity develops around this.

My calling has allowed me to live generously with my neighbors in a way that I couldn't have done previously. Yours can too! Your calling allows you to not only stay focused, but it gives you a purpose that allows you to navigate challenges and obstacles with resilience and determination. When we know "why," we are doing something; this sense of commitment provides more power than passion, willpower, or ambition alone.

When we are destined for something, there is no such thing as failure. Roadblocks, obstacles, timing, and our what or how may change, but it's the why that pushes us through to victory.

Calling Snares

At 14, my son barged into the house like a bear, screaming, "I got it!!! It worked!!" He was ecstatic. He walked in, rabbit in hand. His snare was a success, and he was looking forward to cooking up a rabbit dish for his lunch.

At this point, he had been researching snares and trapping methods for about a year or so—

reading about it, watching videos about it. It was his passion. And this day, he became a trapper.

A snare is a common hunting tool used to capture an unsuspecting wildlife victim. Snares are hard to see and generally placed in the direct path on which an animal travels often, called game trails. If the animal sees the snare or catches the scent left on it by the trapper, it will avoid the area.

I find snares to be a great analogy for the things in life that trip us up. These are traps we want to avoid, which aim to keep us from fulfilling our callings. They typically lay in wait, unnoticed, in the form of a misconception—something we believe to be true but that is based on a fear we hold. Let's look at a few of these kinds of "snares."

1. "If I am called to it, it will just happen."

Here's the problem with this thinking: just because it is a calling doesn't mean you don't have to work for it. Like maturity doesn't come with age, callings are not set in stone. They are good for you to aspire to, but you must receive them. Think of them more like a gift. You can choose to receive one and open it, or you can choose to return it to the giver. Once you receive it, you can choose to store it or use it. Pursue your calling!

2. "I don't have the plan finalized."

When you are called to something, you probably don't have the plan fully set. Even if you do, it will likely change, but start anyway. Start with what you have. In time, you will have your calling revealed. It doesn't always come at once. Sometimes, taking a step is necessary in order to see the next step on the staircase to your calling.

3. "I don't want to screw it up."

You may fear making mistakes. That is normal, but God thought of your stupidity (and mine) when he gave us our callings. Not having the plan and not wanting to screw it up are both fear-based excuses. They feed off the unknown. Do it afraid! Following the calling on your life will be the best and most rewarding decision you make in your life. It allows you to design a life you don't want to vacation from.

4. "What if I look stupid?"

First, recognize that everyone starts somewhere. You can't get yourself caught in the comparison trap; it will paralyze you from making progress. To some people, you will look like a crazy person. Those aren't your people. Remember the movie *Field of Dreams*, where the voice says, "If you build it, they will come." Your people will come and they will thank you for showing up for them.

5. "I don't feel ready."

Nobody feels ready. The doubts you feel will subside once you start. Motivation never comes first. It always comes after you get going. When my wife and I first became parents, I was not ready. I thought I was more ready than I was and it propelled me to become better. You don't know what you don't know and that is okay. If you wait until you are ready, you will never get there.

In order to avoid these snares of faulty thinking, we must power through the terror barrier. This is an invisible wall in our minds that keeps us in our comfort zone and prevents us from growth. Knowing that growth is good and that comfort is not always helpful to us, we must push forward to gain an awareness of our situation and examine whether it is a snare that will trap us or an opportunity that will help us grow.

Character: How Will You Get There?

Calling will get you up in the morning, but character will keep you in the game.

Vision is extremely important, but it is not the most important item a leader brings to the table. A captivating vision will only get you to the first challenge. After that, character becomes the quality that sustains the efforts. I have heard it said that people are like tea bags: you find out what they are made of when they get into hot water. How will you get there sounds like a vision question, but really it is a character question.

> "Character is not a 'recommended optional extra' for a leader; it is a 'non-negotiable' requirement." - Malcom Webber

When we think of character, we often think of good qualities or characteristics we see in people, things like integrity, humility, kindness, trustworthiness, responsibility, respect, caring, morals, and ethics. These qualities are evident in great leaders that we all look up to. Think of someone you admire; my guess is that they embody qualities similar to this list.

As a young leader, a sophomore in high school, I was accepted to be a sixth-grade camp counselor. I can remember the impact my camp counselor had on me and I wanted to do the same for someone else. Unfortunately, I didn't have the same character qualities my counselor had.

It was day two of camp. Counselors were tasked with passing off beads to the sixth graders for being great campers and having great behavior. Singing camps songs as we marched from one activity to the next? Have a bead! Help a camper with a task they were struggling with? Have a bead! Well, I had heard that if you licked a certain type of slug, your tongue would go numb. That must be worth a bead or two, right?

The next morning, all the counselors were called to an emergency meeting. "It has come to our attention that some counselors are passing out beads for things that are dangerous and inappropriate for our campers," one of the leaders announced to the group. Guilt ran through my body. I knew that what I had done was wrong and I had been caught. I felt terrible about it. Not only that, but I could have ruined someone's camping experience—the one single thing that had inspired me to volunteer for this opportunity to begin with! They graciously didn't single me out in front of my peers. The leaders knew that the staff's accountability would help to steer my character. It did and I learned a great lesson that day about influence and that leadership is not something you should wield to manipulate others.

There have been many debates that, and philosophers who, have held views on leadership and whether leaders are born or made. The truth is more complex than one or the other; leaders are both born and built. Why do I say that? Well, some leaders are born into families with strong leaders. They seem to have better leadership qualities right out of the gate. Personality traits through genetics absolutely play a role in leadership style.

That being said, leaders are grown. Like in the story above, I have also seen, in myself, my ability to lead increase by the development of my character. I believe anyone can be a leader and that we are all capable of greatness.

Why do I bring up all this about character in a conversation about generosity?

Character is built through adversity. The toughest times in our lives reveal our true selves. When we reflect on that, we can allow our conviction to push us to better, higher ways. When our character is developed and strong, we exhibit traits that are congruent with generosity, like peace, patience, gentleness, hope, joy, kindness, goodness, faithfulness, perseverance, self-control, and godliness. Generosity is the act of being both kind and plentiful. These character traits allow for generosity to flow freely and are marks of not only a good leader, a leader worth following, but a healthy and whole leader.

Character Snares

Just like the snares that try to keep us from pushing forward in our calling, there are similar traps that grab us on the path of character development. Here are some common character snares that stand out:

1. "It's too hard."

Yes, it is hard, but it is not TOO hard. It is costly, but it is worth it! Anything worth doing is always uphill. Stick to it and keep moving. After going through hard things, you can see that it was temporary and that you made it. This builds resilience. Have faith, in God, in yourself, in others. If you are going alone, it will feel hard. We aren't meant to go alone; if it feels hard, there's usually a lesson in it for you. And above all, remember, you were made for hard!

2. "I messed up and feel ashamed."

You will make mistakes. Acknowledge them, make amends, and move forward quickly. We call this "failing fast." Your emotions of feeling ashamed for making mistakes is normal and it shows that you genuinely desire to do it differently next time. When you know better, you do better. Fear of making mistakes or being hurt can keep you from continuing forward; you lose especially important character development opportunities.

3. "I can do it on my own."

When we have a "Superman" attitude, we miss the ability and opportunity to address blind spot areas. These areas that we can't see, but others can see clearly. Our ego, or pride, often keeps us from addressing problem areas that hinder the development of an extremely important character trait of humility.

Character is necessary for each of us to develop the trust needed to lead anyone. While sometimes the journey of building character can be difficult, it is a necessary one. One that, in time, will prove to be worth every challenge, obstacle, and mistake. When we see the traps in front of us, we know what to look for. Developing our character will lead us in all that we do—in how we spend our time, have relationships, and even how we use our gifts and talents.

Competencies: How Are You Gifted?

Each person has a unique set of skills, talents, and aptitudes that makes them distinctive. These skills may have come naturally to you and they may have been developed with time during a period in your life. Why are these competencies important to living generously? Because these are contributions you can share with the rest of the world.

If one person is skilled in something (Person #1), there may be another person in their life or community who is *not* skilled in that very same thing (Person #2). Meaning, Person #2 NEEDS Person #1 to show up in their life and share that gift. These gifts show up in a variety of ways.

In business, you have people who are gifted in numbers and math and you have others who are gifted with strategy and marketing. You have people who are task oriented and others who are geared toward people. All are necessary and yet not everyone has all the skills and talents at once.

For example, growing up, I was terrified to speak in public.

Fear led me to delaying developing that skill and ultimately pushed me away from something I find that I actually, really love to do.

On the other hand, I have tried to do a lot of things and realized that they weren't for me—

Motocross being one of them. Music was another. Not being able to develop those competencies, at first, sent me into confusion. They were things I loved and wanted to pursue, but for one reason or another, they fell to the wayside. That doesn't mean I don't still love those activities. It just means I can appreciate them in a different way.

Not seeing the competencies of others hindered me from building effective teams. I needed to see myself truly, so I could understand where I needed others to step in and fill the gaps I was creating. Don't' get me wrong; there is nothing wrong with not being good at a specific skill or task. We are all created to have a uniqueness that makes us who we are. But we do need to understand what those areas of uniqueness are and what we will need to mitigate our weaknesses.

Ultimately, finding out what you are good at means you can share it generously with others. Remember, living generously isn't just about money. We can be generous with our talents, time, encouragement, positivity, etc. The areas we are skilled in are often someone else's weakness. Just by being you, you add value to them.

I am an ideas person. I am constantly and consistently hearing throughout my life things like, "I never thought of it like that," and, "What a great idea," or, "There is no way to make that happen." The truth is I always have ideas, lots of them. This is a gift. Once I learned how to use it, it became a great gift that I share with others.

I also do that through coaching. This gift allows me to see things differently and not get pigeon-holed easily. In business, it has allowed me to think strategically and develop unique solutions to complex problems. I can see a challenge as an opportunity instead of a dead end.

> "Leadership is the capacity to turn a vision into reality." - Jim Rohn

It takes skills and character to take a calling and bring it to life.

Snares of Competencies

Calling and Character aren't the only leadership areas of our life that have snares. Competencies also have common snares that keep us from pursuing them and becoming more deeply and fully realized:

1. Discouragement

Parents, spouses, and friends can often be our biggest cheerleaders, but what if they aren't? What if they don't understand your vision and calling? This leads to discouragement. It is especially difficult to have these people become our naysayers because they have influence with us. The voices of our loved ones can often be a snare to the pursuit of our calling. Maybe, it happens as you're making a big decision like whether you are going to go to college or not. Perhaps it happens as you are about to pop the question. Intuitively, you know the next right step. You can seek advice and listen to wise counsel, but you are the one making the call. Don't let discouraging voices fill your mind.

2. Fear

Sometimes, *The devil you know is better than the devil you don't,* you think. I read a book to my kids when they were younger called *The What-If Monster*. It depicts a child thinking about all the "what-if" questions that keep him from doing something new. *What if it's scary? What if they laugh? What if it's hard?* Finally, he has some questions of his own: *What if they don't? What if it isn't? What then?* Fear can try to keep us from doing new things, but when we use our mindset to reverse the question and push through the fear, breakthroughs are bound to be on the other side.

3. "I don't know how."

Perhaps you have hit a wall and don't know where to turn. Seek out a mentor. Someone who has been there and done it. If you have something you're truly passionate about, you will make it work!

4. "It's too much work."

They say it takes 10,000 hours to become an expert in something. If you spend 40 hours a week for a year doing it, that's about five years to master it. The investment is not for the weary. If you are not called to it, this is where that separation happens, most often.

What if all these snares were obvious to you? What if you could see them from a mile away? What if you decided to avoid them and forge a new path? Read on . . .

Avoiding the Snares and Hearing the Sounds of Generosity

When we break through the snares and develop our Calling, Character, and Competencies, we find that generosity is a natural outpouring in abundance. You know what you are called to do, and that you have what it takes and the skills to make it happen.

Generosity is being kind and plentiful to others with grace and mercy. When you know who you are and what you can do, you can stay in your strength zone all day. It's no longer "work"; it's how you were designed.

Think about this: generosity displayed in our lives is like a professional orchestra playing a beautiful song. The notes are played in the right venue with the right acoustics by the right people on the right instruments in the right way at the right time. There are multiple parts coming together to make a beautiful harmony of sounds that delights the auditory senses. When we develop our character, calling, and competencies, it has very much the same harmony in our lives that music has.

Now imagine the sound system through which the music from this orchestra is playing. The sound board has multiple inputs and outputs. Inputs are like a microphone, which records the violin, #2 recording the viola, #3 the cello, #4 the bass, and so on. Outputs would be akin to left main, right main, and sub-woofers. Like a sound system, we have inputs and outputs that make up our life. Character, Calling, and Competencies are the inputs. Who you are, what you are called to do, and the skills and abilities you have to accomplish those things will be the beautiful symphony your life plays. Generosity is the output from plugging the sound system in correctly and equalizing the channels.

Composing Generosity

When his non-profit, First Pursuit, was founded, Neil brought an "orchestra" together, piece by piece. He composed the music and worked on conducting the musicians as they passionately played in sync with one another. His **calling** was to bring men together.

He would develop them by inviting them to do an activity that became a relationship where they knew each other and were able to grow together. His **competencies** allowed him to recognize his own weaknesses and bring people around himself to assist with those areas. His **character** was what allowed him to lead for so many years.

Neil demonstrated what it means to live generously by doing the work of developing himself in the areas of character, calling, and competencies. He has been an amazing friend and mentor to me and I have had the privilege to learn a tremendous amount from him.

Perhaps, in your life, you recognize a calling but feel unprepared or unqualified. Maybe you have a certain set of skills that most people don't know about and you need to start sharing them with others. Or, it could be that you have tried to push forward with your calling and share your talents, but your character hindered your progress. These types of issues are common among people all over the world. However, they are ones that require and deserve our attention. If developed, our character, calling, and competencies will help us make the world a better place. They will allow you to bring an orchestra of your own together and create a magical experience that delights those around you and ignites something deep inside them to become more like you.

You've got the music in you! Let us hear it!

Questions for Reflection and Discussion

This section of each chapter is to help you think through what you have just read and apply it to your life. As you reflect on what you just read:

1. What have you learned in this chapter?
2. In what ways did you use TACT[2] in this last chapter? How will you follow up with those notes?
3. Where are you going? And why?
4. How will you get there? With whom?
5. How are you gifted? Where do you need help?
6. If you could do one thing and could be guaranteed not to fail, what would it be?
7. Does the last question help you see what you're passionate about?
8. How do you need to develop your skills to fulfill your calling?
9. What experiences in your life have helped develop your character?

Chapter 4

EVERYONE WANTS TO BE AN INFLUENCER

Integrity
Nurturing
Faith
Listening
Understanding
Enlarging
Navigating
Connecting
Empowering
Reproducing

I love this acronym of INFLUENCER[9]. It accurately points out what it means to influence others and be a leader who positively impacts those in your care. To be an influencer, it means you are a person of character who has skills, talents, and abilities serving your higher purpose. You are a difference maker!

The journey toward becoming an INFLUENCER starts with awareness, which is what the first three chapters of this book were all about. Now, we will begin to explore taking our awareness and becoming intentional in the context of relating to others, and how we apply the act of generous living.

Becoming a person of (authentic) influence—i.e., leadership—doesn't come from a desire to influence others; it comes from a desire to make a difference. However, this is often easier said than done! Most of us have three major problems when it comes to influence. First, most of us have only seen fractured models of good leadership at best. Second, thanks to the recent growth of social media, we tend to think that, in order to be an influencer, we need a large following. And, third, we think we don't have the time. Let's tackle each of these three obstacles individually.

Solution to Problem 1–If You Don't Have a Model, Find One

When we don't have a model for good leadership, we have no frame of reference for it. Just like babies are brought into the world, they must learn EVERYTHING by watching and seeing it modeled repeatedly. Then they begin to practice it many times over. I hate to break it to you, but we are all, in fact, just big babies! The lesson for them applies to us because *we don't know what we don't know.*

Even worse, some of us have had NO model for good leadership; we've had overtly NEGATIVE models in our families of origin. Annika, for example, shares this story:

> *"I was blackmailed and intimidated into staying silent, fully knowing I would never be able to speak of the hor-*

rors in my home if I wanted to live to see another day. A day came, though, where I no longer cared about living another day. I no longer had hope for a better tomorrow. With suicide notes written and my mind made up, it is only by the grace of God that the very day I planned to take my life also happened to be the day I was placed into the foster care system.

There I stood, at 17 years old, in the middle of a busy grocery store parking lot, just a stone's throw from my high school, fresh blood encrusting the deep cut just under my eye, my breath as white as clouds in the chilly Oregon night air. The headlights of passing cars driving sent waves of pain into my black eye, and my body was as stiff as could be, frozen by fear unlike anything I had ever felt before. On May 24, 2010, with just the clothes on my back as my only personal possessions, I became a ward of the state of Oregon as case #IK73509.

A whirlwind of emotions warred within me for not only the following few weeks but also the years that ensued. When you are removed from all you've ever known, however bad or good it may be, it is absolutely traumatic. Though I was placed in a physically safe home, that feeling of 'safety' was not something I had known for over a decade prior. I trusted nobody—except for myself. Though food was always available there, I always felt like there'd never be enough for me. Though I was never alone in that home, I always felt like I was fending for myself in this life; I was meant to figure it out all on my own.

My behaviors reflected those of a terrified child: flinching at every sudden movement, bursting into tears at the drop of a dime, and guarded with walls so high it was impossible to get close. At the core of me, though, that same terrified little girl just wanted to belong.

I dreamed of having a mom who would squeeze me when I needed a hug, who would teach me how to be a young woman, and a dad who would keep me safe and stick around to show me not all men were out to hurt me as I had experienced before. I dreamed of parents who would pray for me, advocate for me, and cheer me on.

I felt anything but worthy of my dreams—but in the depths of my heart, it was truly all I wanted."

My friend Annika (Annie) is an extremely creative young woman with a keen eye for photography. She is gentle and mild. Just by looking at her, you would never expect to learn of the trauma she has endured in her life. Deep down she is fierce. Her love is strong, and she has tremendous passion. She is a warrior and has a support network that is strong and caring.

When we lack models, we need others, like Annie's foster parents, to demonstrate what authentic leadership needs to look like. As Annie shared in her story above on the blog *Lovewhatmatters.com,* our need for belonging never ends.

We all have a deep-down desire to be loved. To be known. To be safe and experience an abundant life full of joy and happiness. Just like Annie, the rest of world is searching.

Bono talked about the search in his hit song, where he says, "I still haven't found what I'm looking for." We all know the feeling, but why is it that we seem to be looking for a microwave answer in a gourmet kitchen? We cover the void in our lives with bandages to hold ourselves together while we attempt to solve the problems on our own.

Like Annie, what we need is someone with experience to show us how to make it happen. To continue with our analogy of the microwave answer in the gourmet kitchen, we need someone with experience to show the way around the kitchen. We don't need the chef; we just need someone who has been in the kitchen and seen the process.

Imagine standing next to Gordon Ramsay as he coaches you to make a four-course meal. Would you have the skills to help support the chef and be picking up or refining your skills to become better, or would you be falling behind and frustrated because you don't know what you don't know? If he is a good coach, like he has proven to be in the kitchen, he would meet you where you are and challenge you repeatedly until, eventually, you could replace him. That's what good leaders and mentors do.

We need someone with experience who we can learn from and grow. Who is that for you? Who are you doing that for?

Solution to Problem 2—Start with What You Have

Now, let's look at problem number two. The "go-big-or-go-home" mentality has created a barrier in our minds that we need to press through. YouTube, Instagram, SnapChat, TicTok, Twitch, Twitter, Facebook, and other social media platforms have reshaped how we think about influencers. We see people who are amassing a large number of "followers" on their pages in an attempt to have major influence. If we dig a little bit, most of us feel we need a large following or platform like that in order to influence people.

What we need are people who show up to make a difference, people who positively influence those around them with Integrity, Nurturing, Faith, Listening, Understanding, Enlarging, Navigating, Connecting, Empowering, and Reproducing themselves in others. We need people who are less worried about how many and more concerned with how impactful. When we understand and embrace this attitude, our altitude rises higher.

Start with where you are and with what you have. It doesn't have to be big; it doesn't have to be elaborate—you just have to decide you want to make a difference.

Solution to Problem 3—Make the Time

Problem three is our greatest excuse: *I don't have time to volunteer, give back, get involved in, etc.* Someone I know is notoriously saying they don't have time to (fill in the blank). These excuses are nothing more than a lack of wholeness. We haven't prioritized things in our life. We don't have margin.

The reality is that we make time for the things we value, but when we are poor or lacking, we tend to feel like we have less control over these things, but it is still true. If someone says they value their family, but is rarely home, you have to question what it is they actually value (hint: it's the thing that's taking them away from home).

Take a moment to inventory your life and assess where you spend the most of your time, and with whom. Be honest. Do your actions reflect your stated value?

The Impact of Influencers

> "Leadership is influence, nothing more, nothing less."- John C. Maxwell

Think about it: parents, friends, teachers, and people can all have a profound impact on us. I am sure you have someone in your mind right now, who has influenced you. It could be a good influence or a bad influence. But someone has impacted you by influencing you at one point.

If leadership is influence, that means if you have influence with one person, you are an influencer, a leader. That is HUGE! When we embrace this simple truth, powerful things begin to happen. Understanding this puts us on a path of growth as we begin to recognize the gaps between where we are and where we would like to be. Recognizing that we have the power to make a difference, even a small difference, will help motivate that growth because we want to be the best version of ourselves in the lives of others.

The truth is that people of this world deserve to be led well. And, in order to lead others well, we need to be leaders worth following.

Annie's story didn't end with hopelessness and an aching desire to be loved. She continues her story with this:

> *"It has taken me years to find my voice, to know I can speak up, and to use my voice to advocate for others. As a youth in foster care, I ached for a family to be a part of. I longed for a mom and a dad to do the rest of my life with. I craved for a reality where forever, permanency, and*

security existed. I never outgrew the dream in my heart to be adopted.

Being adopted at 26 created a foundation that changed everything for me. As I continue to walk the healing journey, I have parents who will always walk right beside me. I have met so many family members and family friends who have taken me in as their very own. I never have to question my place to belong."

Annie's, and that of her amazing adoptive parents Adam and Jinnalee, is a story of redemption and love. It's a story of two people who knew they wanted to make a difference and, by offering a place of healing and mentorship, i allowed Annie to grow in an environment that showed her just how much she matters. It's a story that has revealed to her that she is loved, and nothing can convince her otherwise.

Annie found what she was looking for. A family. Amazing people she could look up to and learn from. People who would be in her corner and influence her to live a life of positive impact. But she didn't stop there. Now she has taken what she learned to the next level by advocating for others. She is giving the very thing she needed so badly. She can positively influence children who are going through so much and connect with them, because of her past, and guide them to a better future.

When I think back to my own story, I can relate to some of the feelings Annie shared. I wanted to be loved and feel secure. I had a deep fear of abandonment, and insecurities I would carry into my adult life, fears that I would have to wrestle with and come to terms with to start a process of healing and wholeness.

I can recall a few special times that I got to spend time with my dad, 10 to be exact. One time I was about 12 or 13 years old.

At the time, I loved Motocross. I thought that was going to be my career, my life. On this particular day, I was in a panic! I had just popped the rear tire on my 1992 Honda CR80 the day before I had to race—travel day. On the three-and-a-half-hour drive, we stopped at a local parts store to pick up a new tube and proceeded to the track. This particular race was at Washougal MX Park in Washougal, Washington. It was one of my personal favorite racetracks on the circuit.

When we finally arrived at the track, it was dusk and the sun was already casting bright orange streaks on the grass and trees. We got our campsite set up and my dad went to work on my rear tire. He was a mechanic by trade, and he was good at his job. For some reason, he was struggling with putting the innertube in. I was sent out to call him into the camper for dinner. He said he would be there in a minute. I never saw him come in. He worked well into the night. In the morning, I woke up to a race-ready machine.

I don't remember much about racing that day besides the fact that I was nervous that he was watching me. I wanted to make him proud.

On the way home, I found out that he hadn't slept at all. He had spent all night putting a new 12-inch inner tube on my 14-inch tire. Somehow, the wrong tube had ended up in the wrong box. Whether it was a manufacturing error or a customer return, we will never know. However, I learned a bit about what kind of dad I wanted to be that day.

My dad had an all-or-nothing mentality. I can understand not wanting to be a part-time dad. I know there is a complex story there that I will never know. What I do know is what happened out of that. A need was developed in me, a deep desire to be the dad I never really had—the one I had glimpses of, but who never really modeled the full deal.

Help Is a Good Thing

Two weeks after my 21st birthday, I met an amazing person. I didn't know it at the time, but she was someone who would teach me more than I could have ever imagined. Someone who helped prepare me for some of life's biggest hurdles. Someone who helped me realize my influence and the great weight and responsibility of the role as an influencer.

I had waited a long time to meet this person. In fact, I had literally dreamt of this day for years! What would she be like? Would she like me? Could I help her?

The answer came in the form of my now-wife, Jackie. And the day finally came when I could be the help for her I always wanted to be.

Jackie was eight months pregnant at time. We went into the hospital because she was having pain. It would come and go. "Probably false labor" they told us.

During the 30-minute drive to the hospital, I had asked Jackie if she wanted me to stop off for some dinner. She wasn't hungry, but I stopped off and grabbed each of us a sandwich anyway. I knew how these things usually went! I thought to myself, *We either stop now or we don't eat. And I want to be prepared before she gets hangry.*

Thankfully, I ate my sandwich on the way there, because it did turn into a long wait at the hospital. Jackie was having a tough time. This definitely wasn't false labor! She couldn't get comfortable. She was trying everything to ease her pain; she would lean over the hospital bed while standing on the floor then move to a large workout ball and rock. She would pace back and forth. It seemed like nothing was working. Finally, the nurse offered a warm bath.

"Okay," Jackie said, wanting anything to ease her muscles. She had been in the bath for about five minutes when she told the nurse that it was time to get the doctor.

The nurse said, "No it isn't; you aren't ready yet."

A second nurse came in and checked. Jackie was already dilated and pushing. The second told the first nurse to call the doctor in quickly. Within 15 minutes, Jackie was in so much pain that she was dry heaving. But then it happened.

There was a brief period where the earth stood still. A still calm at the end of it all.

On December 11th , at 4:11 p.m. our son was born, and our world changed. He was four weeks early and exactly six pounds. He was so little and helpless, laying there on his mom. What an amazing day, I thought! I have been waiting for this for a long time!

It only took about a week before I realized I'd had no clue what I was doing. I was stressed. I was tired. I was not trained. I was not prepared. But I gave what I had, and it was enough.

Talk about on the job training!

The Power of Influence

I was so FAR away from where I wanted to be. As I look back, that was one of the best revelations because it allowed me to set out on a path to become the father, person, and leader I had always wanted to be. Now I just needed to learn how to navigate the gap between where I was and where I needed to go.

Out of the realization of my need, I was able to recognize that I needed help. Leadership is a big responsibility, something that we shouldn't take lightly. It carries a lot of weight and therefore should be treated with a level of respect and admiration. I heard someone once say that authentic leaders never desire leadership; they desire to make a difference. That is so true!

In Kevin Hall's book *Aspire,* he shares a story about how he went into a shop in Vienna, Austria, looking for a gift when. There, he was taken aback by the shopkeeper, Pravin Cherkoori:

> *"The shopkeeper's eyes widened at the mention of famed Viennese psychiatrist, Holocaust survivor and author of* Man's Search for Meaning. *'I knew Victor. He was a great and noble man,' Pravin said with admiration, at which point he reached beneath the front counter and produced a large leather guest book. 'Viktor, like many others who have passed through Vienna, signed this Book of Greats.'*
>
> *He leaned forward as he opened the book and placed it on the top of the counter directly in front of me and said, 'Kevin, you are one of the greats. Will you sign my book?'*
>
> *I looked at the names on the pages. There was Dr. Frankl, and Mother Teresa, and members of Mahatma Gandhi's family.* This man has just met me, *I thought,* I felt unworthy of signing his book. *Certainly my name didn't belong alongside such distinguished company.*

After pausing for what seemed an eternity, I responded, 'I appreciate the compliment and your thoughtful gesture, but I do not believe that I am one of the greats. I'm sorry, but I can't sign your book.'"

Pravin begins to ask Kevin what he believes they have in common:

"I didn't need to think long about my response. Words my mother taught me since I was a child echoed in my mind. Without hesitating, I replied, 'I believe that you are my brother. We were created by the same Creator. We are part of the same human family.'

My Indian brother relaxed back in his chair and exclaimed, 'That is what I believe also!'

From that moment on our conversation took on a depth of personal interest as if we had broken new ground and understanding.

Pravin spoke about his early years. 'I grew up in Calcutta,' he began, 'among the poorest of the poor. Through education and hard work my family was able to break the shackles of poverty'" After a pause, he resumed. 'My mother taught me many great things. One of the most important was the meaning of an ancient Hindi word.'

That brought me to the edge of my chair.

'In the West you might call this charity,' Pravin went on. 'But I think you'll find this word has a deeper meaning.'

What word could have more depth than charity? *I thought.*

Speaking deliberately, almost reverently, he continued as if he were revealing a sacred secret.

'The word is genshai,*' he said. 'It means that you should never treat another person in a manner that would make them feel small.'*

I pulled out my leather journal and wrote the salient word genshai *(Pronounced GEN-shy) and its meaning as taught by newfound friend.*

Pravin continued, 'As children, we were taught to never look at, touch, or address another person in a way that would make them feel small. If we were to walk by a beggar in the street and casually toss him a coin, I would not be practicing genshai. *But if I knelt down on my knees and looked him in the eye when I placed that coin in his hand, that coin became love. Then and only then, after I had exhibited pure, unconditional brotherly love, would I become a true practitioner of* genshai.

Chills ran up and down my spine as I sat speechless, reflecting on the power of what I had just heard.

'Kevin, you are truly one of the greats,' my host pro-claimed, as he motioned toward me with his hands. 'But you refused to sign my Book of Greats. When you made that decision, you treated yourself small. Genshai *means that you never treat anyone small—and that includes yourself!'*[i]

Not only is this a great lesson about how we should live, but it's also a great lesson for all of us in what it means to positively influence another person and live generously. It first must begin with us, within us. It's an attitude.

As an illustration of influence used in the best way possible, Pravin took Kevin on a journey to understanding something very important about himself; he also showed him how he could go and do the same in the lives of others. Pravin and Kevin weren't lifelong friends; they had just recently met. But, it didn't take long for Pravin to gain some influence with Kevin through mutual connections.

Pravin didn't let what little influence he had with Kevin be an excuse to not do anything. He used what influence he had to help Kevin become an even better version of himself.

The Takeaway

There are a few key takeaways I would like to expand on from each of these three stories: Annie's adopted parents with her and her with the children in foster care whom she advocates, my dad with me and me and my son, Pravin with Kevin and Kevin with the readers of his book.

At the core, there are some common connections that tell an important story, a story that can be a guide to you on your journey of influence. Thinking about these stories, there are a few simple words that come to mind: guide, mentor, leader, influencer, generosity.

Each of us has influence; influence begins with understanding our value and becomes powerful through valuing others. Influencing others is a responsibility we hold dear as leaders to lead generous lives as we influence others to do the same.

When we understand that we have influence, the next question becomes, *How should we use it?* This is living generously.

That question cannot be answered simply in this book. It can only be worked out in your own life. If you are struggling with *how*, start with the *why*. The *how* will come naturally to you.

Questions for Reflection and Discussion

This section is to help you think through what you have just read and apply it to your life.

1. What stood out to you in this last chapter?
2. In what ways did you use TACT[2] in this last chapter? How will you follow up with those notes?
3. When did you realize that you have influence with others? What is that story?
4. Who has influenced you?
5. Whom do you have influence with?
6. How can you increase your influence with the person or people in the previous question? Give an example.
7. How can you lead with generosity right now? Give an example.

Chapter 5

INTENTIONALITY

ere's a puzzle for you: What is a non-renewable resource that is often taken for granted, can "catch up with you" or "get away from you," elicits feelings of longings for more of it, and has inspired countless books, movies, philosophers, playwriters, songwriters, scientists, physicists and more?

The answer is: time.

When we are young, it feels like we will never be old enough, but as we get older, it seems that time slips away faster with each trip around the sun! God has given everyone equal measure of one of the most valuable resources to use it daily lives. No matter the color of your skin, how old you are, the nation you were born in, the clothes you wear, which part of the world you live in, or even if you are male or female—we all have the exact same amount of it.

We are each given 24 hours. No more, no less!

While we know this is true, there is something drastically different about each and every one of us when it comes to time—that is, how we view time, how we use time, and how we give our time.

I think we would all agree that the time we have is precious. Every second the clock ticks is a moment now in the past. Time is a non-renewable resource that cannot be saved or resurrected. Once it is gone, it is gone.

With the average lifespan of 71 years, we each have an average of 2,240,589,600 seconds of this priceless resource during out lifetime. If we were to knock off the first 20 years of our life as we navigate our calling (a very conservative number), and six years off the back end so we can enjoy a relaxing retirement at 65, we are left with 45 productive years. One-third of that is spent sleeping, which drops us to 30 years. Now, we plug in a few assumptions based on national averages:

Watching TV, movies, or streaming takes off three hours per day.
Two and a half hours a day are spent scrolling social media.
One and a quarter hours per day are spent eating and drinking.
Nearly two hours per day are used cleaning and doing household chores
One hour per day is spent on shopping (groceries, Amazon/ online, clothing and household items, etc.)

When we calculate all the hours spent doing these things and subtract them from the 24 hours in a day, we find that we have only six and a quarter hours left out of the day. We spend eight hours a day, five days a week, working. Forty hours a week, divided into seven days, is around five and three-quarters hours. That leaves us with barely more than half an hour a day!

I know that life is busy (and that was a lot of math!). But bear with me on this line of thinking. Many things in life jump out like a deer in front of the car on a dark night. They are unexpected, take time to deal with, distract us from what we were originally doing, and cost us valuable time and money.

If we don't have margin in our life, a little extra time to spare here and there, we can be totally blindsided by these events.

With this understanding, it is of the utmost importance to discuss how we spend our *time* and how it either fosters or hinders our ability to live generously.

How You Spend Your Time Reveals Your Priorities

We all wake up each morning wanting to win. We need to take that intention to the next level by acting on it. Merely desiring to win isn't enough to make it happen.

How we spend our time is an indication of two things. First, it gives us insight to what we truly care about. And second, it can be indicative that we are trying to avoid something in our lives.

For example, taking some time to get ready in the morning shows you care about yourself. Spending *too* much time getting ready, on the other hand, can reveal we are trying to impress others.

Watching a show or movie every once in a while can be a relaxing and enjoyable experience. On the other hand, spending every evening binging your favorite streaming platform may indicate you are avoiding something in your life.

See what I mean? Use of time can be subtle, but it can also be obvious.

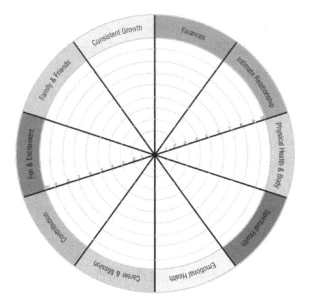

There are eight primary areas where we spend our time, as the "wheel of life" shows in the above illustration. The wheel of life is a tool that helps us visually assess our current fulfillment and find balance in these areas of life. Many times, this is used in coaching to help clients see areas to which they may desire to give more attention, and areas where they need to continue doing what they are already doing. It doesn't matter if you are a business professional or a stay-at-home mom.

Think about it this way: what you do with your time is how you redeem it. To "redeem" something means to regain possession by means of payment. How we use, or redeem, our time is one of the most important lessons we can learn.

Let's say we have room in our family life section of the wheel where the results can improve dramatically. If we were to look back on how we redeemed our time, we would find we weren't investing much time to that area, specifically. We may have felt like we were home with the family, but perhaps our focus was elsewhere. This is common in all of us, especially when entering new seasons of life.

There are many things going on in your life—some obvious, some not so obvious. There are areas of confusion and chaos mixed in. Neither of those are helpful with regard to redeeming the time. If we are confused, we don't know which direction to go. If there is chaos, it may seem that every direction could be right because the idea of getting out of the chaos, no matter the direction, seems paramount.

If redemption is simply buying something back, then how do we buy time? It belongs to us already, doesn't it? Well, I guess that depends on how you view time.

How We View Time

Some of us view time as if it will always be there. We will get to the important stuff tomorrow. What I have learned is that tomorrow is not a guarantee. Everyone who died today had plans for tomorrow.

Others view time as if everything is under their control. They have their days planned to a tee. Their calendar is packed with tasks and looks like a well-oiled machine. Time is money, right? Well, sometimes the most important thing isn't on your calendar, like the time needed to invest in your relationship with a spouse or child. Perhaps they only get part of the weekend and some vacations now and then.

There are two thoughts I have in relation to how we view time. The first one is seeing time as an opportunity and not something that just ticks past every second. The second is that everything is temporary. Let's start by looking at viewing time from the standpoint of every second being an opportunity.

> "In every day, there are 1,440 minutes. That means we have 1,440 daily opportunities to make a positive impact." - Les Brown

Each moment in time is a choice, an opportunity. Our free will, given to us by our Creator, has allowed us to choose how we use it. Do we choose to buy back our time for good or allow it to tick past without a second thought?

You may be reading this, thinking, *Well, I don't set out to do wrong things. I do my best every day.* Think back to earlier in this book where we discussed mental wholeness. Remember our thought life is where so many of our decisions are made! We have so many reoccurring negative internal thoughts that not doing something positive is choosing to let negative win. Time is much the same. When we don't buy back the time with good, we are *allowing* wrongdoing, which is essentially the same as *doing* wrong.

> "He who passively accepts evil is as much involved in it as he who helps perpetrate it. He who accepts evil without protesting against it is really cooperating with it." - Martin Luther King Jr.

Let's be honest: each of us allows things we shouldn't. We do things we shouldn't. We hurt those we love. We say things we shouldn't. We try to do the right thing, but we fail. If you are like me, you fail . . . a lot. More than you would care to admit.

I believe you are right in thinking you try to do the right thing most of the time. I do too. I don't believe anyone wakes up thinking about how they are going to fail, hurt someone, or make a mistake. Like I said earlier, all of us wake up in the morning wanting to win.

Failure isn't always a bad thing. Failure helps us recognize our need. We also must recognize we are imperfect, requiring something more than ourselves. However, when we see time as an opportunity, we can learn to forgive ourselves for our missed opportunities or failures. We can see that the next moment is here, and we can move forward to redeem the next opportunity.

The second thought I have in relation to how we view time is that everything is temporary. Another way to say it is that nothing is permanent. We tend to think of the various circumstances or seasons of life as permanent while we are living them. The reality is there is only one thing in life that is permanent. That is death.

"I wish it need not have happened in my time," said Frodo.
"So do I," said Gandalf, "and so do all who live to see such times.
But that is not for them to decide.
All we have to decide is what to do with the time that is given us.[10]"

- J.R.R Tolkien

In life, we go through various seasons. Sometimes we feel we are hindered in living generously because of the season we are in. When my wife and I were in our twenties, our middle daughter, Lily, needed 24-hour care. She was worth every second of it, but my wife and I both operated in a way that caused us to feel trapped. We couldn't commit to hanging out or doing much on a regular basis because it was difficult to ask for sitters. We burdened ourselves with the brunt of the load and didn't invite too many people to help us carry it.

Sometimes the weight we feel on us is so strong that we can't live generously. You know what? That is okay. That just means we need to get healthy first (refer to Chapter 1). Here's something I want you to know and something I wish someone had told me. There are people around you, who want to help, who want you to win. People who will pour into you and help you in your need if you would be generous enough to open up to them. When we see things as temporary, or as seasons in life, it helps us to invite others in for that moment in time.

What we say we value and what we demonstrate we value can be two very different realities and sometimes can cause us to rethink our lives a bit. This happens a lot with prioritizing. There are always a multitude of matters that pull for our time. Sometimes many of them are worthy causes. However, sometimes we also need to learn to say no to good things so the best things can happen.

How We Cash In Our Time

Do we choose to buy back our time for good or allow it to tick past without a second thought? Using our time is either taking advantage of the opportunities in front of us or allowing them to slip by without identifying or taking advantage of them. I am not suggesting we must be intentional with every second of every day. That is not practical or reasonable. Even if we were to put forth our best effort, it would be impossible. What I am suggesting is, just like a budget working best and most efficiently when it accounts for every cent, we account for our time.

Redemption of my time for good is what I strive for—"spending" it wisely. Redemption is an action word. It means we aren't just *intending* to do something; we are actively participating in *doing* it.

On my way to work one morning, as I was driving on I-405, a car had its blinker on to get over in front of me. I slowed but he didn't take the opportunity to get over. As I drove past him, I noticed that all he was doing was looking in his rearview mirror to see what was coming up behind him. He wasn't looking out his window or side-view mirror at all.

He hadn't noticed the substantial gap I had left for him to get ahead of me because he was so busy looking behind him. His inaction left us both frustrated.

I use this to illustrate a common pitfall in life when it comes to redeeming time.

You see, it is impossible to redeem the time if you are missing the opportunities waiting in front of you by being focused on your past or the past mistakes of others. We must forgive ourselves and allow God to forgive us of our past, so we can move forward with our future. We can use time best when we are focused on the time we *will* spend rather than being focused on the time we have *already* spent.

The most fascinating thing I have learned about time is that some people can seem to do amazing things while others can't seem to get much of anything done. Why is that?

Intention with time plus action in real time equals redemption of time.

Intentionality + Action = Redemption

Your success is not determined by what you *intended* to do; it is established by what you *actually* do. There is so much generosity that needs to happen in the world that there simply isn't enough time to do all of it. I know you're probably thinking we live in a busy time as it is, and here I am making a case for you to do something else with your time. So, what do we do? The answer is that we need to prioritize the right things.

Redeeming the time is not as simple as it may seem at first glance. While I love and use the wheel of life as a tool, I do find it is incomplete. It identifies many important aspects of our life; however, it is missing our spiritual life. In my experience, this is the number one most important aspect that informs all the other areas.

You can think of it like the heart or brain of the body. When it isn't functioning properly, the other areas are impacted. There is a reason the first of the Ten Commandments in the Bible—"You will have no other gods before me"—is first. It isn't because God has an ego problem. It is for our benefit and His glory.

Your relationship with God must come first. Allow God to examine your heart and mind. If we are putting God first and allowing Him the room to do this in our lives, it establishes a posture and attitude in life that it is His time, not ours. If God is not first, life becomes a means to an end and very self-serving:

we use people to get what we desire. We listen to respond rather than listen to understand. We do whatever it takes to ensure our desired outcome is satisfied.

If, on the other hand, God is first, it leaves us in a position for fulfilling the opportunities that come our way to serve others. Our motives always become clear. If our minds or hearts are poisoned with pretentious motives, the evidence is in how we use our time.

Deciding to redeem the time for good, and putting God first, allows for the ultimate good: the redemption of how we will be intentional with the time allotted to us in service to others.

How We Give Time

Time is the most precious non-renewable resource we have. When we show up to a birthday party, a graduation ceremony, a wedding—any event for someone else—it is using the most valuable resource we have that cannot be returned. When we do something for work, we are exchanging the most valuable resource we have for a paycheck. We are always giving our time.

For a period in my life, I kept telling my wife, "I've got to quit volunteering for everything. I'd be a millionaire already if I got paid for everything I volunteered for." What I hadn't learned yet was this: busyness doesn't equal productivity. My focus was not on others, but on myself and what I should get for my time, energy, and intentions.

How you give your time has to do with the grace in which you are extending your most valuable resource. This isn't transactional. It's transformational. While transactions are taking place in exchange for time, we need to understand the fuller and bigger picture.

When we are living life on purpose, success is inevitable. Is your life merely an existence or is it about purpose, meaning, values, and passion? Are you going through the motions or enjoying what it is every moment of the day? That's what makes having a life worth living and especially a life worth living generously!

I encourage you to prioritize what you are being called to do. The truth is, we make time for the things that matter to us. Read that again. It may be a tough statement to hear, but a necessary one to let sink in. Focus on God and identify your calling—and how you give your time will become clear. Sure, there will be challenges. There will be tough times. There will be times where we make poor choices. But knowing what you are here for— your calling(s)—will help you prioritize your time.

In order to live a life packed with richness and fullness, we must understand and embrace *ourselves*. Jesus said part of the Greatest Commandment is to love our neighbors as ourselves (see Mark 12:30-31). That's right—in order to rightly love others, we must love our *self* properly first! What are our values? What are our goals? What makes us feel fulfilled and living with passion? What gives life meaning? How do we live in harmony with others? How do we move past failure? Are we growing? All these are great questions we must wrestle with.

The truth is our callings matter. Many of us struggle to find our calling or struggle with the process to fulfilling it. Not everything is clear, and that's okay. I like to use the image of a staircase in the fog. It is so foggy you can only see the next step. Sometimes that step may seem a little hazy too, but the staircase is your life and fulfilling your calling. The fog is the noise and the chaos of life that hinders your eyesight and focus.

Take the next right step and trust the process. Our calling will dictate our time and ultimately how and what we prioritize. When we are living in our calling, the things we do aren't necessarily work; they are a piece of something that brings us fulfillment and joy.

Take this story, for example. My friend Patti is a real estate agent and had a young client couple from out of state who were purchasing a home. For the sake of the story, let's call them Chuck and Mary.

Mary had just been promoted and they needed to relocate for her new job. Chuck was finalizing things back home and gearing up to meet Mary to get this deal closed and begin a new chapter in their lives.

Patti, in normal fashion, had spent a ton of time with them over the previous few months and had made sure their buying experience was unmatched. She didn't simply work to get the deal closed; she went to great lengths to show Chuck and Mary that they mattered to her and were a priority for her. She had written several offers and this one had finally been accepted. The couple seemed thrilled to close this deal and enjoy the new home.

That is, until one night, about 3:30 in the morning, Patti received a phone call that woke her from sleep. "Why would they be calling me at this hour?"

She must have muttered it out loud because Patti's husband, Dennis, responded with, "They are probably pocket dialing; just go back to sleep."

She went back to sleep. The phone rang again. She couldn't help but feel that they were backing out of the deal. Was it something she had done? She tried to put that out of her mind, and rolled back over to fall asleep again.

Ring! Ring! 5:30 a.m. this time. Something was up. Patti got up and listened to the first voicemail. It was Mary. Chuck had had a severe seizure. They were in the ambulance headed to the hospital together. The paramedics had suggested she call someone. Patti was the first person who came to her mind.

She listened to the second voicemail. "Chuck has passed," Mary said through the sobbing.

Patti immediately cleared every appointment on her calendar and raced to the hospital to be with Mary. She couldn't get there fast enough. They cried. They prayed. They grieved. Together.

At the hospital, the nurse had asked Patti how she was related to Mary. She responded with, "I am not. I am her real estate agent." The nurse gave Patti a look to suggest she was shocked at the notion and replied, "Oh, you guys must have known each other for quite some time."

"No," said Patti, "Only a few months."

In Patti's mind, she was thinking, *Isn't this what anyone else would do? Why is this so out of the norm?* But the reality is, it *is* out of the norm. Most people would not cancel their life to put another person first who wasn't immediate family. This truly is the Good Samaritan story in our day, a story of someone who saw an opportunity to redeem the time for good and give that to someone who was in need.

If we look at this story from Mary's perspective, we can imagine how lost she feels. Alone in a new town, she is experiencing tragedy and heartache, and needs some form of security to help her through. She needs to cling to something or someone that has a firm footing. So, she calls the person with whom she has built a rapport, someone she can trust. That is Patti.

If we look at this story through Patti's perspective, we see she is working a job she loves and that gives her personal fulfilment. She has chosen to live out her values. Just look at the lengths she goes to for her clients, to make their experience match her personal values.

How does she show up for Mary? She cancels all her appointments for the day to spend it (and many more) with Mary. She may not have all the right words to say. She may not be able to turn Mary's situation around that day, but her presence as someone who cares enough to show up is enough to set a spark in her and influence Mary in a positive way.

Patti has just "bought back" (redeemed) the time for good by living out her calling.

When we live out of our calling in life, impact is something that happens along the way—

just like how, in this story, Patti thought her response was normal, but it looked odd to others that a real estate agent would drop everything for a client. The impact happened because Patti knew her calling, and was willing (and happy) to give her time to it.

The impact you have in life will stem from how you buy back your time. And, just as we saw with Patti, the purpose and calling on your life will, then, reveal itself to others in how you are living.

Time, they say, is the great equalizer. What sets us apart from others is how we view time, how we use time, how we give our time, and what we give it to. Begin buying back time for good, then evaluate: look back on your day each night and reflect. Look back on your week and reflect. Do the same with your month, your year, etc. This built-in time of reflection is vital to our growth. If we aren't doing it, we are missing a huge opportunity that is right in front of us, opportunities to live generously and impact others.

Living on Purpose

We live in the busiest time in history. Often, we are grabbing fast food while we are on the way to practice for one of our kids sporting events after an evening commute from work. We build lives in which our calendars are maxed and we think we are being productive, when the reality is . . . we are just busy!

We are an on-the-go people.

The passage of time helps us realize we have a limited amount for everything we do in life. The difference between busy and productive is simple. Busy is having a full calendar. Productive is having a return on investment.

My wife Jackie and I have been on a journey to design a life we don't want to vacation from. One where we are each operating in our strengths and passions. A life that is lived on purpose, with purpose, for a purpose. It is created in everyday, ordinary moments, but trust me, they add up and then begin to multiply.

You can too! It begins with taking one step and then taking the next right step on the journey. You can do it!

Questions for Reflection and Discussion

This section of each chapter is to help you think through what you have just read and apply it to your life. As you reflect on what you just read:

1. In what ways did you use TACT[2] in this last chapter? How will you follow up with those notes?
2. What did you think of when you were reading about intentionality in your life?
3. What is on your calendar? Why?
4. Do these events serve your purpose?
5. How will you redeem the time today?
6. What does it mean to design a life of purpose?
7. What step do you need to take next to bring that design into reality?

Chapter 6

OUR RESPONSE TO GENEROSITY

E ach of us has unique responses to generosity in our lives. Individually, we have different ways we express generosity, and we have various responses when we receive generosity—depending on how we are living, our past experiences, our current circumstances, our current mindset, and what we are doing.

Some people take advantage of generosity. Others feel unworthy of generosity. I believe we need to use a situational approach rather than a blanket ("one size fits all") approach. Remember, it's all about relationship!

Sugar-and-Egg People

My wife and I decided and made a commitment to each other that we wanted to be the "sugar-and-egg people" in our community. The idea is that we would be the family in our neighborhood that our neighbors would walk over and feel comfortable to ask, "Could I borrow some sugar?" We wanted to be the hub. We wanted to be the house in our community that people could count on, not just in times of need, but especially in times of need.

We made this commitment to our neighbors too, but it wasn't verbalized; it was just acted out over time. In our interactions with our neighbors, through conversations, we would hear of a need we could meet and offer a helping hand.

One time, a neighbor mentioned needing to go on an errand, but had her hands full with her husband being deployed. We immediately offered to watch her kids while she went out. Another time, we had a terrible windstorm. The evergreen limbs covered the ground, reminding me of a battlefield from a battle that had been lost the night before. The limbs were everywhere. Nearly every inch of yard was covered. Our neighbor was across the street loading limbs into a small trailer. We walked over with a chainsaw, gloves, and a rake to help.

What we found out through doing this was that most people would like their neighbors if they just got to know them. We aren't talking the nods and waves from walking the dog or driving past each other in the neighborhood, where there isn't much interaction. We are talking about actually *knowing* them— knowing what they like, dislike, where they work, what their kids' names are, and eventually inviting them on a camping trip.

Getting to know your neighbors is the biggest hurdle. Everyone has their own things going on. They come home from work, drive into their garages, and you don't see them emerge. If you live in Washington, like I do, that can be a nine-month season! Our goal has been to get to know our neighbors well enough that we can get together during that nine-month period, in each other's homes, and be comfortable doing so.

This doesn't happen by accident. We had to create opportunities to engage with our neighbors. We decided to make a Christmas gift for each of our direct neighbors, meaning the neighbors with whom we shared a property line. It wasn't extravagant; it was simply a plate of goodies. However, it gave us a reason to knock on their door and start a relationship. Not every neighbor was as receptive to our generosity as others, and that is okay. What happened is that we have developed some amazing friendships by doing this.

This illustrates how each of us has a response to generosity. When something generous happens, it can change our lives. It changes how we see others. It doesn't have to be some epic event or a grand gesture. It can be small and still have a significant impact.

The Response

My wife Jackie has been on the pursuit of wholeness with me, which I talked about in Chapter 1. Her challenge is to make sure she is giving from the overflow, and not only serving. (Serving is great, but it shouldn't deplete us of all our energy.)

For what seemed to be years, I had been trying to help her see the balance between serving others and ensuring that she wasn't giving from an empty cup. She has a servant's heart and sometimes allows it to get the best of her, like what I experienced with my mom during my childhood.

For example, instead of sitting down to watch a movie as a family, she would be doing laundry or cleaning something.

Knowing that reminding her it would be there later wouldn't be helpful for her, I would tell her I would take care of it so she could come and sit with us.

One afternoon, she had gone to the mall to have what I will call a "yes" day for herself. She bought herself a new purse that wasn't falling apart. She got her hair cut for the first time in over a year. And she was able to get a massage and relax for a bit. I was pumped to see her take the initiative to make this happen!

Just the day after her yes day, she turned to me as we were driving in the car and said, "I received the nicest compliment at work the other day. A customer said, 'I love coming here!' and told me I was so genuine, and that they felt I actually cared about them each time they came into the shop."

She was beaming! If that smile was sunshine, I would have been blinded and crashed the car. Seeing her this happy from a compliment was so great! It led me to begin thinking about the bigger picture. This customer didn't have to say anything. They could have just gone about their day and kept the thought in their head. Their act of generosity to my wife was confirmation of two things for her: First, that she needs those moments in life, the yes days, to reflect and recalibrate. And second, it allowed her to recognize that she is impacting people by being her genuine self with each interaction, and that they are noticing a difference between her shop and other places.

Jackie was transforming strangers by being herself and genuinely caring for them. That's because when transformation is experienced, it can't be kept quiet. When people have a unique experience, they share it. This is why reviews sites like Google Reviews, Yelp, Trip Advisor, and the like are so popular. What we are really after isn't reviews though; it's testimonials. Testimonials are evidence of transformation.

Testimonials come when something has happened that transforms or impacts a person. They have either experienced or now understand something new or in a deeper way. Something inside of them has been impacted so dramatically it changes how they think, or something has happened to them that changes the way they perceive the world.

And, when people have been transformed in this way, it often inspires them to live generously. When we experience personal transformation, we are able and wanting to share transformation with others and impact their lives! It's a beautiful thing!

So, what is keeping us from this kind of living?

I would say this: generally speaking, we don't like to step out of our comfort zone. We want to avoid being uncomfortable. Paying a neighbor a visit when you have lived in the house next door for longer than a few months can get uncomfortable. Offering a compliment to a stranger can make us uncomfortable. Anticipating people's needs can also be out of our comfort zone, especially if we have a more introverted personality style. Surrounding yourself with likeminded people who encourage and lift you up will help you break through the terror barrier, but you will still have to do the hard work of making the decision to go after something more.

Break through the Barrier

Imagine an invisible electric fence that keeps you locked in your backyard. Inside the fence is your comfort zone. Outside the fence is freedom. You can see beautiful landscapes on the horizon. To your left, you see large mountains. To your right, a beautiful blue ocean. In front of you is a field of wildflowers as far as your eyes can see. Behind you is a charming forest that captivates your eye and inspires you to explore. You want to experience each of those things, but you cannot seem to get past that fence, no matter how much you desire to. You have tried jumping it, digging under it, and even running through it, but every time you try, the shock of the fence keeps you in.

The comfort zone is a vicious place in which we often find ourselves. The only way out of it is to break through the terror barrier. But how?

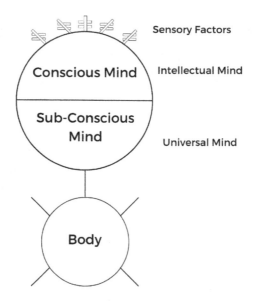

This is an illustration depicting stage one of a concept developed by Bob Proctor, called the Terror Barrier. It reveals an amazing truth about why we tend to operate in a scarcity mindset rather than an abundance-driven mindset.

The conscious mind is directed by the sub-conscious mind. The way we have experienced life, over time, through our senses, informs and develops our sub-conscious. These are the things we believe to be true, regardless of their validity. That is why it is called the "program": X experiences equal X thoughts equal X actions.

If we want to break through the terror barrier (fear) we will need to adopt an attitude of "doing it afraid":

I can't.

Worry.

Doubt.

Fear.

These are symptoms of living in the comfort zone. My guess is you have had to deal with your fair share of these feelings. I want to help you tap into something better. In order to do so, the idea of doing it afraid will become your motto. When we resolve to break through the terror barrier, it doesn't mean we don't feel fear. It means we don't allow the feeling of fear to keep us from doing it anyway.

When I started my sophomore year of high school, it was a requirement to begin working on a three-year assignment called a senior project. This project was about our career choice after high school and what we were doing to prepare for and pursue it. The presentation was basically telling everyone what your plan was after high school.

I had NO CLUE what career path I should choose. I had NO CLUE how to plan or prepare. I also knew I would have to give a presentation of all of this during my senior year, in order to graduate. Just like I had no clue what I wanted to do after graduating,

I also had no clue about the concept of the terror barrier. This is stage one of the terror barrier: recognizing the concept.

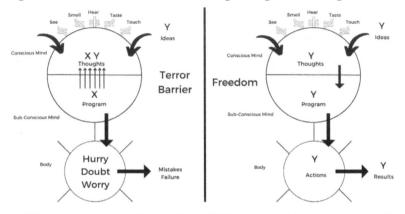

The second stage is one in which an outside idea comes into our minds. *I want to see the ocean over there, I want to explore that forest, I want to smell those flowers, I want to quit my job, I want to start my own business, I want to be a stay-at-home parent, I want to "Y."* This outside idea comes in and we have a choice to make. We can entertain it for a moment and, as soon as it makes us uncomfortable, put it out of our minds. Or, we can face the fear, push through it, and go after what we truly desire. Do it afraid!

My sophomore year went by. I was nowhere closer to knowing what I wanted to do. I had not been pursuing anything career wise and had no plan to. How could I present something I knew nothing about? Fear filled my soul. So, I did what any rational person in my situation would do. I transferred high schools, so this project was no longer a requirement to graduate.

Fear can make us do all sorts of irrational or desperate things.

These days, it doesn't help that we are living in challenging times. We are still unsteady as a society, coming out of the

COVID-19 pandemic. The stock market has been increasingly volatile over the past few years with all the implications of businesses closing, markets shifting, and wars and tensions between countries escalating. There are a lot of situations and circumstances that can allow fear to hold the driver's seat and throw us right back into our comfort zone. We take on a scarcity mindset that tells us to hunker down there and stay safe.

This scarcity mindset is like playing a game of musical chairs. We go through life fighting for a seat and waiting for someone to knock us out of the way just before we sit down. It causes us to be on guard and to protect our comfort zone rather than push through to the other side. This is no way to live!

It's not hard to understand why we want to stay there. Economically, the world seems to be on the edge. It appears we are dangling over a cliff and the ground is cracking beneath our feet. You may be reading this, thinking, *How in the world can we believe in abundance in a time like this?* Partly, this line of thinking is based on what you are experiencing right now. When it seems the world is experiencing a level of scarcity unparalleled in our lifetime, it is easy to slip into the idea that we must hold onto what we have. I assure you, pushing through these fears, breaking through the terror barrier to freedom, is much more rewarding than you can imagine.

I would flip the question and ask you this, "In a time like this, how can we *not* live generously? How can we *not* have an abundance mindset and give hope to those around us?"

Scarcity tells us that you can't have both. It is a mindset of either or. The world doesn't generally seem to play out in the way of abundance, in our experience. People are looking out for themselves. They are staying in their comfort zones. However, when we create genuine impact moments, by living generously and having an abundance mindset, it can change the world around us simply by gifting others a unique experience that opens their eyes to something greater than what they have known previously. In doing so, we are showing them a new reality, one in which they can also participate.

There are a number of television shows out there where someone takes a broken and rundown house and transforms it into a beautiful home. In a world that is broken and falling apart, wouldn't it be great if we came together to fix the broken pieces and restore it? We need fixer uppers like Chip and Joanna Gaines to help us fix this house! We need to break through the terror barrier and go all in.

From Impact to Significance

My friend Mike Newman lives for impact. He is a coach, trainer, mentor, teacher, leader and someone from whom I have learned a lot in the time I have known him. He is always adding value to those around him.

On one occasion, we had just wrapped up a conference called Elevate. It was a large lift, financially, for which Jackie and I took most of the brunt. Mike put in countless hours helping to develop a successful conference.

If you have ever tried to pull off something like this, you know it is a lot of work. If you haven't, let me assure you, there are so many things that go into it that you don't even think of— right down to deciding what color the napkins should be!!

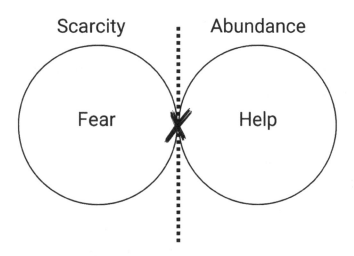

For a first-time conference, it went way better than I was expecting. (I am a very optimistic person, so that's saying something!) While there were a lot of things we learned, I walked away from the event knowing it had been successful. Our little team did an excellent job pulling this big event together. Afterward, I was reflecting on how amazing that experience was and how thankful I was to lead it. About three weeks after the event, I received this card in the mail:

Robert and Jackie:

I sit here at my desk this morning, thinking of the impact you both have in the Puyallup Valley. Your faith is amazing! There is so much in store for you as you faithfully follow God's lead. The venture into Elevate was a huge investment of time, energy, and resources. You carried the load and risk of the financial resource. You both should be proud of the way the Elevate conference was received by our attendees. It was a huge success!

Sometimes our investments take time to reap the results. Seeds are planted. God will grow them. I am using this check to invest in you! Thank you for your generosity, this means a lot. Keep pressing on.
Mike

Inside the card was his honorarium check, taped to the inside front cover.

Now, let me tell you a little something about Mike. Mike has been a coach and a mentor to me, personally. He put in just as much time, energy, and effort to make the Elevate conference come to life as I did. His act of belief and generosity went beyond impact to significance because this wasn't the first time Mike had poured into us.

Impact is great: it is the result of good leadership and pursuing the best for others, but Mike's influence has helped me see there is even something better: significance.

We all want to leave our mark. We desire to have impact in the world and leave a legacy that will inspire others. This is a noble goal. I believe this is also a noble path to get to something even greater. When we create impact in the lives of others, we are creating an experience that informs how they view the world.

Significance is what happens when our impact is compounded over time. Don't grow weary while you are doing good! This is a helpful biblical reminder for us that can adjust our attitude and keep us focused in the right direction (see Galatians 6:9). Each moment of impact created compounds over time and becomes significant.

I know a man who failed several times before he found success. He went bankrupt within one year of starting his first business. His next business failed when he relied too heavily on one single company for his revenue stream. When they closed, his business failed as well. After that, he found himself fired from his next venture for not being creative enough. Then he made a poor business deal and ended up walking away from the business entirely. He lost control of the intellectual property and decided to try again somewhere else. This person was none other than Mr. Walt Disney.

Walt's life, as we know it, was most certainly not a failure. In fact, he had a very successful career. The difference between Walt and others is that Walt kept going. Where most others would have given up, Walt persevered. Can you imagine the things Walt was hearing? The people around him were probably worried for him. Wanting the best, they pushed for him to give up on his dreams.

But Walt didn't let his failures define him. Because of that, he would accomplish many of the visionary dreams he set out to do over the course of his life and career. All because he didn't give up.

If you look up significance, you'll see Walt's smiling face, right there in the dictionary, reminding you not to give up too! He is famous for saying, "The difference between winning and losing is most often not quitting."

It can be so tempting to quit, to allow the unknown—the things we can't see, the work happening inside someone else—to pull us out of the work we are doing, simply because we can't see it happening. Be patient and keep going. The part you are playing in impacting the lives of others is shaping their story too. Don't forget that! When we live generously, others see the genuine and authentic generosity that flows from us. They recognize something is different. It takes time, as with all things worth doing.

Generous Faith

Each generous act buys back time for good, but it also redeems the future.

I'm sure we have all seen the 1985 Robert Zimeckis classic, *Back to the Future,* and the sequels that followed. Do you remember that trilogy? If not, stop what you are doing and go watch them, like now. Right now!

Welcome back! Now that we have that out of the way, and the films are fresh in your mind, we can continue. Throughout the trilogy, a recurring concept is explored where we see how the actions of the characters impact time. What one character does in 1955 affects life in the future of 1985. For example, when Marty McFly saves George from getting hit by the car and gets hit instead, that one action throws his entire existence into question. Or, how about when Biff brings back the Sports Almanac in the second film? That one action created an alternate 1985 where Biff was a millionaire big shot and Hill Valley was corrupted.

While there is clearly a difference between reality and the movies, the biggest difference here is that we can't go back and see what the various outcomes will be based on our actions. Therefore, if we want to live in the "ideal" Hill Valley scenario, we will need to take the best actions we can in our circumstances. That makes me think of a couple of local business owners who learned about redemption of the future.

Lori was a dental hygienist who became a small business owner after many years of working part time alongside the woman who started the business she would end up owning—a quaint, British-themed grocery store and café. Mike, her husband, is from the UK and had always felt like Americans weren't very community centered. (Especially living in Washington State, known for the "Seattle Freeze," a term used to describe the difficulty of making new friends in the Seattle area.) The shop was their contribution to strengthening a sense of community in our small city.

Mike and Lori had been traversing one of the toughest economic challenges as they navigated their business through shutdowns, mandates, and other COVID-related hurdles. While the ability to get people into a local small business is challenging enough, now there were newly added obstacles in their way.

Out on a ship for five months—that's where Lori finally located her delayed, perishable order from the UK for her shop. This order had taken what was left of her savings, around $10,000. It was a loss, and the shipping company was not taking the blame for not delivering her order. On the water it sat—pallets full of waste that were going to be goods she would sell to make an income for her family.

Now, when things get desperate, most people don't reach out for help. It often takes someone coming alongside to act and change the course of history. One of Lori's family members did just that by creating a donation campaign for them which raised just over $3,600.

While a great start, there was still a long way to go to offset her total loss. That's when the local Chamber of Commerce jumped in. They rallied around this business and partnered with the local business community to launch a dinner party fundraiser. In that one night, they raised nearly $5,000 and created awareness in the community of Mike and Lori's small business and its needs.

This story redeemed the future of this couple and their family, but that's not all. It also restored their faith in humanity. When things like this happen, it sets us all up for brighter days!

Brighter Days

I believe the world will be changed if more of us would simply live generously. If each person treated others how they would like to be treated, the world would be a radically different place. Love would be abundant, and grace would be plentiful.

Living as the sugar-and-egg people on your block or in your neighborhood.

Mike Newman's generosity.

Puyallup's way of supporting and encouraging Lori.

These are three examples of what happens when we live generously and create significance in the lives of others. You likely have a story of making someone's life a little brighter too. What is that story?

There is a great saying that goes like this: *The world is full of amazing people doing amazing things. And if you can't find one, be one.* Sometimes, we get bombarded with negative things in life (and in the news). We have a choice to wallow in that negativity, or to lead ourselves and others to brighter futures, no matter how bleak the situation may seem. There is always a brighter future available, if we are willing to take the lead and share it with others. My friend, John Maxwell, wisely states, "Leadership is influence, nothing more, nothing less." If you have anyone in your life, you are a leader to some capacity.

Now that we know that, we can say that within your sphere of influence you are there for a reason: to make life better. To help them see their value and their potential. To teach them something about life, maybe even how to live generously.

Influence is easy. All you have to do is use it, live it, and be the example. People are always watching and will take notice. We influence from one heart to another heart, not from mind to mind. And you are here to be you and use your experiences, talents, and calling to teach, encourage, lead, and equip others. You hold the key to positive influence in your community. Stick that key in the door and turn it!

There are brighter days ahead, my friend, and your impact in the lives of others is multiplying the hope for brighter days for them and creating significance in this world. Keep going!

Questions for Reflection and Discussion

This section of each chapter is to help you think through what you have just read and apply it to your life. As you reflect on what you just read:

1. In what ways did you use TACT[2] in this last chapter? How will you follow up with those notes?
2. What do you do when you approach something new or difficult?
3. What is keeping you from your dream of a better future?
4. How can you push through the terror barrier?
5. How are you helping others accomplish their dreams?
6. Who are three people whom you can help reach their dreams?
   a. _____
   a. _____
   a. _____
7. Who are three people who can help you reach your dreams?
   a. _____
   a. _____
   a. _____

Chapter 7

BECOMING A GENEROUS INFLUENCER

ave you ever bought a new car? It doesn't have to be brand new, just new for you. It's such an awesome feeling!! I remember thinking how great I felt driving my new car off the lot. It was a 2007 Toyota Matrix (yeah, super rad!). Fifteen years later, that car is still running strong, I might add.

There were two primary reasons why I purchased that car. First, I could parallel park it without worrying about crashing into another car. It was a hatchback, so the bumper was basically six inches past the rear window. And second, because it was unique. To my surprise, as soon as I started driving, I started seeing them everywhere.

In my brain, I tried to make sense of it. Why did this car get so popular all of a sudden? Turned out, it wasn't any more popular. It was that I began to focus on it. As I did, I would see them everywhere. What you focus on expands.

What happens when we focus on what *generosity* looks like? When we examine genuine generosity, there are common themes that emerge between the acts, as we explored in the beginning of this book: abundance, sacrifice, communication, and service. On the surface, generosity looks like ridiculous kindness toward another person. In reality, it looks like heaven on earth. I hope that, throughout this book, you have seen examples of generosity displayed and modeled.

Learn to Ask the Right Questions

Questions help us to understand. Failure to ask questions can become a regret. And, not asking the right questions will stall the learning. When I think about learning something, I have found that in order to understand the subject deeper, it helps to ask questions—especially questions that will give different answers than questions asked previously.

When we are introduced to someone, we ask questions like, "What is your favorite movie?" To ask your wife of 10 years that question means you have likely stalled out on learning about her somewhere along the journey. The key here isn't just asking questions. Asking *good* and *appropriate* questions opens doors for new and deeper understanding.

In looking at generosity, here are a few questions I would like for us to explore:

- What does it look like?
- What does it feel like?
- What does it sound like?
- What does it taste like?

- What does it smell like?
- Where does it live?
- What type of people does it hang around?
- What color is it?

I can hear you now: *These questions are neither good, nor appropriate in understanding generosity! What are you thinking, Robert?!*

I'll be honest, I almost didn't include these questions in this chapter, that is, until I asked them. We don't tend to think of generosity in these terms. However, I have found that deeper levels of understanding come in learning when we ask different questions. Sometimes those questions may sound like they don't belong, but my guess is, if we ask them, we may have a different understanding that opens new doors for us. If we want something to be different, something must change. Perhaps the questions we ask is a good place to start, questions that deserve to be answered in order to give us a richer and fuller understanding of true generosity.

So, what does it *feel* like?

When I talk about how generosity "feels" when we experience it, what do *you* think of? In my mind, I imagine it's like the feeling of falling in love. When my girlfriend, now wife, would look at me with those eyes that told me how important I was to her, I could see she wanted to be around me. That was such a great feeling. Generosity feels like someone lifting you up after you get knocked down, like someone giving you an amazing compliment. It's that feeling of empowerment you get when you start to build confidence to take on the world.

My wife makes some of my favorite foods. My mouth is watering just thinking about it. When I think about what generosity might *taste* like, it takes me right to the dinner table with her. Have you ever eaten something so delicious that you knew the chef put a lot of love into it, like my wife does? I think of my friend, who owns a bakery in Tacoma called Spilled Butter Desserts, and everything I have had from her little bakery does the same thing for me. The question you must ask is, *Why is that?* Generosity comes out in all sorts of ways—sometimes you can taste it!

Then, where does it *live*? Generosity lives in the hearts and minds of each of us. Does it come out of the house? My friend Chris Robinson is notoriously always saying, "Get out the house!" to get people motivated and moving to chase their dreams and aspirations. If you don't move, nothing happens. If the seeds of generosity live inside you, get out the house, my friend!

Whom does generosity hang out with? Generosity hangs out with generous people. Studies have linked generosity to activating the same reward pathways as eating and sex[11] —two things that will not only never go away without the demise of humanity, but also two things known to, under healthy relationships, create well-being and overall health. When good behaviors in our lives are rewarded by our brains, they get repeated. Then, they spread to those around us. Generosity spreads by hanging around generous people.

What *color* is it? This may be one of the more abstract questions. Some people probably begin to think of green because that's the color of money. Others may think of it as yellow because that is the color associated with happiness. There's a reason the traditional smiley face is yellow. Perhaps it's blue, because you see generosity as building trust with others. Maybe it's red, to symbolize the hunger that is satisfied at the table when you host people for dinner. When I see generosity, it is colorful. It isn't any one color. It is all these things and more. My friend Kyle Rogers put it this way: "Generosity is like a cornucopia overflowing onto a table. It is bursting with color and vibrancy and entices those who look upon the table."

Once we know what something looks like, what it truly looks like, we begin to understand it more intimately and we begin to see it everywhere.

HELP! I Need Somebody—Not Just Anybody

One of the problems I have faced is that, no matter how much I try to understand something on my own, I still find I often fall short in terms of its fullest meaning. It really does take other people to help us see the whole picture. When other people begin to share about something, a new perspective is formed.

It's a funny thing, help. We love it when people ask us for help because it affirms we have something to offer and it makes us feel good to be needed. Generally, though, we don't like to be the ones doing the asking!

We want our lives to change in some way, because we are stuck in a rut, but we can't find the courage to ask for help. Here's the truth: if we want something to change, we will have to change something! As we discussed earlier when we talked about the terror barrier, changing things is difficult. We must humble ourselves enough to push through the fear of asking for help and push through to the other side, so we can grow. While growth starts with personal development, the next step is recognizing that we need others.

Personal development goes to the next level when we humble ourselves to seek help outside of ourselves. Help can be a therapist to help with your past. A mentor to share their experience and insight into how they did something you are looking to model your idea or concept after. A coach to break through barriers that will help you take next steps to reach your goals and accelerate your timeline. A conference, a book, a podcast. Whatever it is, we all need outside help. I want you to seek the help you need in your current situation.

This person may be a parent, a teacher, a friend, or a professional. Find them. Maybe you don't know what you need help with. After all, if we don't know what we don't know, how can we know? Start right where you are. Start by simply sharing with someone that you don't know where to go, what to do, what you need, etc. This will allow space for them to ask you questions that can point you in the right direction.

Think about life. You start out as a baby and grow into an adult. In the beginning, you need support 24/7. You can do very little on your own. You need someone to feed you, clothe you, change you, hold you, talk to you, love you.

As you grow into a toddler, you start doing things on your own. As you become a teenager, you gain more independence, but still have much oversight with teachers and maybe a first job. As an adult, the opportunity for you to care for yourself is yours, not fully, but primarily.

Then you hit marriage and you must consider another; parenting takes that to a whole new level. You and your spouse each have a built-in accountability partner in the other to humble you if you won't do it. Once the kids are out on their own, they start having families and you can share with them what you have learned.

Do you see that humility is built into life? We need others. You can try all you want to do it on your own, but I assure you, you will find that you quite simply cannot.

Here's a truth bomb for you that my friend Tony Duck casually said during a conversation that I wanted to make sure I passed on to you: "There is NOT a lack of information. What we have is a lack of guidance." Pause and reflect on that for just a moment. We live in a time where we can go online and find a tutorial for just about anything you could imagine. Why is it that we don't seem to have a dramatically significant increase in successful people?

The reality is, we need someone to go the way, and show the way, as they go.

The Leadership Square

A model that captures this concept has helped me a great deal: the leadership square. While it is quite simple in concept, it is rich in depth, and quite an effective tool. This model shows us the process of going from learning to leading. It is a process of being invited into something and learning how to do it for ourselves and then leading someone else as we teach them how to do what we learned.

Now, before I share the leadership square, let me say this: my guess is that you have not had the privilege of someone walking you through the full process. While it is widely accepted and many organizations have adopted this model, many people rarely see it practiced all the way through. This is a common mistake, but it is detrimental to both the leader and the follower. When seen through to the end, you have fully trained someone in the what, how, and why instead of just pieces of the task. When done in part, it leads to the leader being frustrated that they aren't measuring up and the follower discouraged and looking elsewhere for help.

There are many reasons for people to not take someone fully through the square. Sometimes we feel like things are easier for us to just handle them and that it is more work than it is worth to show someone else how to do it. Other times, we assume everyone knows what we know. And sometimes, we just don't know how to teach it. Whatever the case, we must decide to break the chains holding us back and commit ourselves to practicing the model of the leadership square.

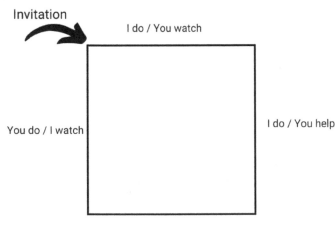

The four-sided leadership square combines the idea of situational leadership theory with a catchy, easy-to-remember learning process. The first corner (top left) is the invitation to the square. This is where someone says, "Let me show you," or, "Follow me." This invitation brings you to the first side of the square. This side is the "I do, you watch" side. This is the first step in the learning process. Someone must invite you in and show you by example.

Something similar happens in a family. When a child is born, they are welcomed into a family, and they pick up on everything like a dry sponge dunked in water. They begin to absorb the motions, sounds, mannerisms, culture, and uniqueness of their parents and siblings. Proximity is the key here. The more time spent together, the more they are picking up. Depending on the situation, this step is sometimes years long and/or doesn't require anything other than the parents being the example.

Situational leadership theory says the leader meets the student (or follower) where they are with what they need—meaning the leadership style changes based on the situation and circumstances. This process is key when transferring leadership from one person to another.

When you get invited into the leadership square, you are never just an observer. It may feel like it, but sit tight! Don't move through the square too quickly. It is often a temptation for people who are action oriented, but trust me, when you soak up the process you will be thankful you didn't try to do it on your own too soon. As you work through the process, you are getting an idea of what is required, the basic steps, how long the task takes, where to find the items that you will need, who else needs to be involved, etc.

In step two of this first corner, "I do, you help," the leader is actively helping navigate and coaching through the challenge of the task as you do it. The leader could be quite literally speaking their thoughts aloud. They could also be expecting that you will start chipping in and getting your hands dirty. Here, you want to make sure you ask lots of questions because you know, at some point, you will be on your own. This demands we fully grasp all the information we possibly can.

Perhaps the leader has delegated part of the task or project to you. All the while, they are sharing insights:

I do this because x.
I am looking for y.
Once that is like this, then I do z.

Confidence begins to grow the follower. This brings them to corner number two, one of the most pivotal points on the journey. This is where most people stop.

Corner two is where, when the task is hard enough for the learner, they can get discouraged and want to quit. It is pivotal as the leader to help by encouraging and empowering them through this time. This can involve reminding them how much they have learned so far and that it's normal to feel that discouraged at this point. You can remind them that the task will eventually become second nature for them once they do it enough times. As a leader, this could be a great time to share your personal experience during this phase when you went through it. This will also build the trust needed to move them to the next phase.

The next step in this corner of the square is, "You do, I help." This is the moment when leadership has been transferred to the student. They a feeling a sense of ownership and are charged with doing the task. The good thing is that the leader is still right there helping and assisting along the way.

This is almost like the apprenticeship situation where the journeyman lets the apprentice lead. For anyone familiar with the trades, the apprentices must be with a journeyman for a period of time to assist with the project. At various times, the journeyman will give the apprentice tasks to accomplish and check up on the work. If they did it right, great! If they don't, they have a review of what isn't right and they get to do it over again.

The time has arrived to do the task on your own as you reach the "You do, I watch" step. Of course, they aren't alone. The leader isn't too far away. The leader is observing and watching, but giving room to learn and absorb all that is required. The leader is there, but the task has been fully given to the student. Innovation and explorations begin, and the student begins to build confidence and make the task their own.

That's the abridged version of the leadership square. It has changed my life and the way I lead. My hope is that you can use it and that it could change the lives of those you lead as well. Chances are, you have experienced very few times in your own life when someone took you through the square fully.

Don't dismiss the process. Don't allow your followers to make the mistake of jumping through too quickly. They could miss out on something very important.

Become a Model
There are certain people from whom we learn what to do. They are people we aspire to be like. They live in a different way.

They live differently because they have experienced something that has changed them. Changed leaders change lives.

From others, we learn what not to do. As we grow and mature, we realize we have an amazing role to play in the lives of others and we get to choose how we show up. The game changes when we realize we are not victims of our circumstances, but rather we have a choice in how we respond to the adversity in our lives. The choice is yours to learn who to follow—not just a mental choice, but a choice that informs how you act. The world is changed by our example and our actions, not by our opinions. Action is where the game is changed.

This is a pivotal moment in the journey of every leader—the defining moment where we, as players, decide how we choose to show up. *What kind of leader do we desire to be? How do we bridge the gap from where we are to where we want to be?* Remember, in order to lead, we must first learn to follow. As we follow, we are learning how to lead. That leader models the way.

As you begin to show up, there may not be anyone following you. That's where you start. It always is. Be okay with that and continue to become the best leader you can be.

I recall, in my journey, starting a Bible study. A lot of work went into preparing and hosting. When only one person showed up, I would be lying if I didn't say that deep down, I was feeling defeated and discouraged.

As I write this, I am planning to speak to over 250 leaders in my community tomorrow. I say that to encourage you! We all start somewhere. Don't allow the disappointments and discouraging moments to stop you from making the progress necessary to become who God is calling you to be.

This is a great time to point out that, physically, growth just happens, but in maturity, that isn't the case. In fact, I know a handful of people who never matured very far. Why does that happen? I think there are many reasons, but I believe we can boil them all to this: we need someone to model our behaviors after. The saying "monkey see, monkey do" is real. We learn through immersion and do what we see modeled, not what we are told. When I tell my kids it's time to turn the screens off, because it's bedtime and I am watching TV or on my phone, it sends them the wrong message. As we begin to grow into leaders, the ones we allow to teach us, guide us, and lead us, are whom we will be like. Learn from leaders who model your "ideal leader."

We often come to the end of ourselves in life. We hit a wall. We don't know how to overcome a challenge. How do we move through the fog when we can't clearly see the path? I have had this happen many times in my own life. It is a process of the leadership square. We need to learn from others and others need to guide us as we learn.

As I write this, I have just finished having lunch with my friend, Karl Newman, author of *The Power of How*. We were catching up on the book he is currently writing and I was asking him questions about the direction he chose to take with publishing because he is about six months ahead of me in the process. If you aren't familiar, there are a few different approaches when it comes to publishing and Karl was in the process of pitching his book to a large publishing company.

We were discussing the advantages and disadvantages of publishing with a traditional publishing house versus self-publishing when the conversation turned a corner and we got onto the subject of building a following (considered a necessity for a successful book launch). I have always had an aversion to building a following because I never wanted fame. He stopped me and said, "There is a difference between fame and influence." Both come with followers, but the motivation for why they follow is the key difference.

People who are after fame may do whatever it takes to get their desired result. People who are after influence are taking the next right step as they impact those around them. Karl helped me realize this simple, but profound truth. We have the opportunity every day to decide how we show up in what we are seeking after. If it's fame, you can find it. If it's influence, you can find that too. But there is a distinct difference between them.

Share the Model (Leadership Square)

Karl had just unlocked a huge internal battle I had been having and he didn't even know it. Just by guiding the conversation and sharing what he was doing, Karl was leading me down the path on which he was already traveling. He was helping me through the process of the leadership square.

Remember when I said there were four sides to the leadership square? Well, that's true, but there is another component to the process. In fact, it is the most important component. That is inviting someone else into the square.

Invitation both marks the beginning and the end of the leadership square. Learning how to lead someone through it brings out a whole new understanding of the process. It is the complete journey through the square, only to start right back up again. This is how leaders multiply themselves into others. This is how generosity multiplies through everything we do: when we share with others, they begin to share with others.

When we serve others, they begin to serve others. When we love others, they begin to love others. We get to share our stories with others. How we were once one way, but now we are different. We get to take people through the process we went through. We get to invite others into a beautiful thing that will help them. As you teach them to do, they will also teach others the same.

Have you heard the question, *Would you rather have a million dollars now or a penny doubled for 30 days?* What has the greater reward? A million dollars is a million dollars and a penny doubled every day looks like this:

0.02, 0.04, 0.08, 0.16, 0.32, 0.64, 1.28.
At the end of week one, you have $1.28.
At the end of week two, you have $81.92.
Week three would yield, $10,485.76.
If you took one penny and doubled it every day for 30 days, you will have a total of $5,368,709.12.

Building leaders can be like this. It may not be until Day 27 or 28 that you realize a penny doubled for 30 days was the right call.

When you build leaders, sometimes it feels like this. Unless I had told Karl what that conversation meant to me, he would have left that day and never known the impact he had. I did tell him what that meant to me.

Let me assure you, if you show up, set the example consistently, invite people in, and stick with it, you will bear much fruit. Continuing to do the work of adding value to people and leading them with integrity will result in a beautiful harvest.

This is just another example of the process of the leadership square, except from the viewpoint of the leader instead of the follower. What is required of the leader is a bit different, because the leader will need to meet the follower where they are. We can never truly know what is going on inside another person, but we can know the process.

The leadership square works and can be trusted. It is the model Jesus used with His students thousands of years ago to create one of the largest and strongest movements the world has ever known. Changing the world starts by committing to the process and building leaders who build leaders. Choosing to start small and making growth, through the process, a habit.

Questions for Reflection and Discussion

This section of each chapter is to help you think through what you have just read and apply it to your life. As you reflect on what you just read:

1. What stood out to you in this chapter?
2. In what ways did you use TACT^2 in this last chapter? How will you follow up with those notes?
3. What are you focusing on?
4. What questions can you be asking to open new possibilities?
5. Who has been a good role model in your life? What made them good?
6. Who has been a poor role model in your life? What made them poor?
7. How can you leverage the leadership square?
8. Who else needs to know about the leadership square?

Chapter 8

WIRED FOR GENEROSITY

One day, I walked into work and had a revelation. At the time, I was working in a giant building with many engineers at one of the largest tech companies in the world.

If you didn't know, when you walk in the halls of a firm filled with engineers, it's . . . unique. Certain industries require certain types of people in order to be successful. It's not better, not worse, just . . . different. *How do you tell the difference between an introverted engineer and an extroverted engineer? The introverted engineer stands there looking at his shoes. The extroverted engineer looks at your shoes.* All jokes aside, I loved the team and the people I had the pleasure of becoming friends with and working alongside of. They helped me learn one of the best lessons in my life and it had nothing to do with my job.

I would walk through the halls at work and, more often than not, observe the tendency for most people to look down and away as we passed in the hallways. This particular day, I created a game to see how people would react if I engaged with them as we passed. It would go something like this, "Hey Eric! Good to see you today!"

Their reactions surprised me. They would get rattled. They would look up at me and the smile on my face as if I had just woken them from a nap or interrupted their deepest thought. The expression on their face was almost like they were reading a manual for rocket propulsion in their mind and I had just interrupted them by slamming a book on a counter. It was during this time I recognized a truth that has served me well over the years—people are different.

One of the ways we can be more generous in life is by embracing this reality. It is not a bad thing to be different. It's not a bad thing to be you. You have been created just as you are, for a purpose. Think about that for a moment. There is not another single person in this world who is just like you and there never has been! You have been created for a purpose that only you can do because of who you are. When we figure out how we are wired, it allows us to express generosity in a unique way toward others, because generosity is expressed through the personal lens of your personality, experiences, and insights.

As we lead from a generous spirit, we not only lead ourselves, but we can lead people well to help them to discover themselves and reach their full potential. As we begin to understand ourselves better and begin to understand others, there is a tool, known as DISC®, that helps us see our unique style. There is wisdom in this kind of self-reflection and analysis that helps us see the truth within ourselves and others. We also begin to see that grace allows room for growth and understanding. We walk a fine line between truth and grace in this, and all things of leadership.

DISC® is an acronym that stands for the four main personality profiles described in the DISC model: (D)ominance, (I)nfluence, (S)teadiness, and (C)onscientiousness. It is a personality style assessment that allows us to understand people a little better, one I use in my business to help leaders better understand their team, and to enable team members to better understand those they work alongside.

People are different, but predictably different. Perhaps you are familiar with Enneagram, Strengths Finder, Myers/Briggs, or another tool that breaks this down. I believe each has a place and holds an important truth. I use DISC® as a baseline for understanding people's personalities—the things that motivate them, the fears they have, and the frustrations they tend to experience with the other personality style.

Let me be really clear: this is not about manipulating people; it is about understanding them and what makes them unique, along with their talents and gifts. This is important to the conversation because anytime we are working with people, there will be challenges and a need for understanding. Understanding where others are, and their perspective, will help us lead others well.

I have mentioned my friend and mentor, Mike Newman, in a previous chapter. He happens to be an expert DISC® trainer and has been someone who has personally helped me and countless others work through DISC® reports and apply it in their personal lives and their businesses. I thought it would be fun to bring Mike along the journey to co-write this chapter together. On top of Mike's personal insights and experiences relating to this assessment, I think you will get a lot out of it since Mike and I both represent different quadrants within the spectrum of DISC®, and can offer our unique perspectives along the way.

What Is DISC?

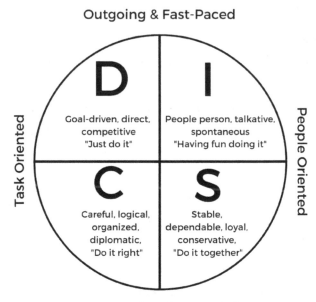

Developed in 1928 by William Moulton Marston in his published book, *Emotions of Normal People*, DISC® was validated and refined during his studies at Harvard University and became what we know and use today as the DISC Personality System®. The four primary personality styles whose first letters comprise the acronym "DISC" are as follows:

- D stands for Dominant
- I for Influence
- S for Steadiness
- C for Conscientious

Here, we want to cover the basics of each style, but we highly encourage you to take the full DISC® assessment and enlist a trained professional help you better understand the results. On page 184, there is a QR code that will take you to an assessment you can take.

Now, in reality, each of us has some varying degree of each of the four predominant personality styles within us. However, generally speaking, one or two—occasionally three—will make their way to the surface as our primary style or style blend.

Two simple questions can give someone a good idea of where a person lands in the DISC ® quadrant:

Question one: are you task oriented or people oriented?
Question two: are you more outgoing or reserved?

Question one puts them either in the right side or left side of the graphic. If they are task oriented, chances are they are either prominently a D or a C. If they are people oriented, they likely have an I or S style. This indicates how they process through their work, by either focusing on the task or the people.

Question two will place them on the top half or the bottom half. If they are outgoing, they will identify with the D or I style. If they are reserved, C or S style.

For example, if they are task oriented and outgoing, they are likely a Dominant style personality. And if they are people oriented and reserved, they are likely a Steady style personality.

Understanding the DISC® model will help us relate better to others because it helps us to realize our own intrinsic relational needs and those of others. Each style is necessary and wonderful. Each style brings out something that the other styles cannot.

While you may have the hardest time getting along with the style that is exactly opposite to your style, remember their opposing style is just different from yours, not necessarily wrong (although it may certainly feel that way sometimes). Fun fact for you: these pairs of opposites generally end up getting married and learning how to work with each other! While it's a struggle, when you can see the strengths in someone else that complement your weaknesses, you begin to realize that they actually both complement each other. Each style expresses an aspect of generosity that the others could not.

D - Dominant style

Dominant personality styles are task oriented. They are outgoing, confident, and assertive. They care about outcomes, not processes. They like challenging tasks that involve risks. The D's greatest fears are to be taken advantage of or loss of control. They can be blunt, stubborn, and insensitive to people's needs.

High D styles value:

1. Autonomy and Freedom

2. Competition, success, competence, and challenge

3. Taking action

4. Immediate results

5. Change

I - Influencer style

Influencer personality styles are people oriented. They are outgoing, talkative, and sociable. They care about having a good time with good people. They are quick to make impulsive decisions and would rather skip the details. The I's greatest fears are rejection and loss of influence. They can take over a conversation and have a difficult time with details and time management.

High I styles value:

1. Fun

2. Relationships and group activities

3. Freedom of expression

4. Taking action, collaborating, and expressing enthusiasm

5. Prestige, attention, recognition

S - Steady style

Steady personality styles are also people oriented. They tend to be more reserved, but they love to come alongside others and help. The S's greatest fears are change or loss of security. They most often will avoid change, confrontation, risks, and being assertive.

High S styles value:

1. Stability and security
2. Opportunities to help
3. Loyalty
4. Cooperation
5. Personal accomplishments

C - Conscientious style

Conscientious personality styles are task oriented, like the Dominant style, but they are more reserved and love to focus on the details. The C's greatest fear is criticism. They can over analyze things, be risk avoidant, and be inflexible with the rules and processes.

High C styles value:

1. Attention to detail and accuracy
2. Expertise and quality of work
3. Thoughtful analysis
4. Stability and control over their environment
5. Personal growth

What Does Each Style Need?

Every personality type has unique things they need each day to feel they have had success in their day. Each style or style blend has what is sometimes called the "Secret Fuel." If they don't get that fuel during the day, they've had a bad day. So often people will leave work frustrated or they will be in a meeting and feel unproductive, because they have not tapped into their Secret Fuel.

For the Dominant style, it is all about getting things done. If they have not accomplished their priority task for the day, over-come a challenge, or have taken on a difficult task, they have had a bad day.

On the other hand, the Inspiring style is all about having fun. If they have not had fun in the day, they will often make their own fun. It may be seeking out a colleague to share a story or a joke. If an "I" style does not have the opportunity to laugh and joke, they have had a tough day at work.

Those are the two outgoing styles of people. When we look at the other two styles, the reserved people, they also have secret fuels that are crucial to them.

The Steady-style folks are some of the nicest people you will ever meet. Their purpose in life, and their work, is to help others. They actually have two secret fuels: peace and harmony. If they have a conflict with a person at work, a client, or someone got upset with them on the phone, they will take that home with them and think about it all night. They will wrestle with the conflict and, until it is resolved, will often carry that conflict with them.

The Conscientious style is the one that likes the details. If they are doing tasks at work that are not focused on accuracy, details, processes, and procedures, they've had a rough day at work. Their secret fuels are quality answers, value, and being correct. They will ask a lot of questions to get the details to understand the issue.

You see, this is about finding what drives the people you lead and how to work effectively together.

My (Mike) style blend is a C/SD. Conscientious, Steadi-ness, and Dominant. Now, when I first went to the DISC training, I was intrigued with the concept of being able to understand people better. Intuitively, I felt I could figure out what drove most people. At the time of the training, I was the Deputy Superintendent in a school district, in charge of business and operations. We had over 4,000 employees. I had eight executive directors that reported to me. I believed I could work with anybody, well, except one person. We were personable and professional with each other, but to be completely transparent, this person drove me crazy. That person was the teachers' association's president and their lead person on negotiations. It seemed that no matter how well I explained things around procedures, processes, finances, and projections, there was always this continuous questioning. It felt like being on the witness stand.

What is my predominant style? C. What is my Secret Fuel? Being correct!

When I went through the DISC® training, the light came on. I began to understand my view, and when the trainer mentioned that the C styles love to ask questions to gain understanding, I had a breakthrough moment. I realized the conflict with the teachers' association president was not about questioning my numbers and data, but about getting clarity so they could share the information correctly with their constituents. Having that epiphany led to better relationships and a less defensive posture with the negotiating team.

What's Your DISC®?

I (Robert) had a big vision of working on a project and was trying to get my friends involved to make it a reality. Being a very high I and high D, I like to persuade and influence people, but I also like to remain in control. This particular project was an effort to build functional proton packs for Halloween, just like in the *Ghostbusters* movies. My first challenge was overcoming them questioning every idea I brought to the table.

"How do you know that is going to work?"

My "I" would want to say that my intuition had confirmed it already. But these two friends happened to be engineers, (who, I was later to find out, generally operate in the "C" style). While I don't officially know their DISC® styles, my assumption was they were CD and CS.

Having high C styles meant that, to them, intuition is garbage; they need data! This required that I beta test some stuff to show it could work. I spent a good portion of my personal time experimenting with my ideas to see if they would work in real life. Let me say, failure is a great teacher!

I couldn't quite seem to get the project to do what I envisioned, the very reason I invited my friends along in the first place. They are *way* more skilled than me at this kind of stuff, but they didn't want to waste their time on something that wouldn't work. We ended up with some pretty terrible-looking proton packs for our first Halloween. Painted foam, fiberglass, bondo, and plastic parts. It looked great for a child's science fair project, but I knew we could do better.

For the following Halloween, I shifted my focus to inspiring them to help with research, something I know they both like to do. They came up with such great ideas, and we ended up with proton packs that lit up just like the movie props and had realistic sounds. We could even get them to play the entire soundtrack as we walked around together. To top it off, we ended up winning a few costume contests and some great prizes that year because of the work we had done. It was SO cool!

For me, the proton packs were a great victory, but the real win was learning how best to work with my friends Eric and Ryan. They taught me some valuable lessons that continue to serve me and help those I interact with every day.

Hopefully you've gone to the back of the book (page 184) and scanned the QR code to access the DISC® assessment and learn what your unique personality profile is. If you haven't, jump on that! Your unique style is not a box you put yourself in. It is not your identity. When we use tools like this, they are there to help us give a picture of how we act and what our motivations are. Think of the DISC® assessment more as a snapshot.

Understanding how you are created will allow you to glean great insight into how you are wired—not only in what you do, but why you do what you do. Whatever your results, when you understand yourself, you begin to recognize that the holes in your style are filled by the strengths of the others. As a D, you may come off a bit too forward, but when you incorporate the I or S styles, they can soften the conversation by bringing in the human element.

Understanding these principles also gives you the ability to meet others where they are and increases your personality quotient. Once you know your spouse is a specific personality style, you can better meet his or her needs, and communication will take a new level of depth in the relationship. The same applies to your manager, direct reports, children, coworkers, classmates, etc.—whatever the relationship, understanding personality styles will help you build trusted relationships and put you in a position to serve them where they need it.

Think about how a master artist has only a few colors on a palette, but when they begin to mix them, there are numerous ways to blend the colors to create new expressions on the canvas. Similarly, blends are the various ways in which each person is created to express their unique style. Because we are more complex and unique, a model like DISC® couldn't possibly capture all the intricacies; we use blends to help capture more of everyone's fullness of style. Blends illustrate the unique contribution of each style we utilize. Like I mentioned, I am a very high I and high D and low S and very low C. That means I am a person of action and don't generally like the details.

When I set out to start a business, there were more than a few things I missed that I wish I had known. First is that I need to hire for my weaknesses first. In teams, you are only as strong as the weakest link. You can mitigate that by hiring someone who operates the opposite of that weakness and in doing so you've just created the optimal situation for success. I scored just below the midline in the Steady style and very low in the Conscientious style. Fortunately for me, my wife makes up the S and C styles that I don't use as often. We make a great partnership!

Teams and Conflict

Partnership, on the other hand, if you give it enough time, always leads to conflict. Jackie and I realized this early in our business journey and knew we needed to set clear roles and responsibilities, so we don't take the working dynamics home with us. I am sure you've experienced some conflict in working with a teammate, co-worker, or employee before too.

Someone dominates a project because they want to move things forward and not bother "talking" about it all day. Another doesn't participate in the project because they don't like micromanaging and feel like their ideas wouldn't be listened to. And another doesn't seem to get anything done because they are gabbing the whole time. Why do we experience these things at work? When you get more than one person in a room, working on a project together for long enough, you will arrive at conflict. Conflict happens for various reasons, but some of the most prominent stem from differing personality styles.

Your unique personality style shows up in everything you do. How you intake information. How you process it. How you give it. And it all informs the outcome.

Personalities impact roles. Roles may or may not be suited for certain personality styles and vice versa. In hiring, it is vital to know what you need, but it's also vital to know how you will work together by either complementing each other or by butting heads. All strengths also bring with them inherent weaknesses.

This applies to any kind of team. Think about sports, for example. In any team sport, it is important to know the rules, the roles, and the plays. In knowing the rules, it is important to have a thorough understanding of them and what they mean. The refs need to know the rules in detail as well as the coaches and the players, but how does personality play a factor in those roles?

If the team captain is a Steady-style personality, they may find it hard to get in front of the team and keep them motivated and encouraged. If the ref is an Influencer-style personality, well, those pesky details? They just went out the window. After all, the game is about having FUN! Each style has strengths and weaknesses that go along with it.

Teams also reveal to us that each style must be present in order to succeed. If one or more of the styles are not present, there will be incomplete understanding of moving the mission forward. What I have found as a leader is that you first realize more work needs to be done and you look to replicate yourself. You find someone who is like you to share the workload. The problem with this is that the work you give to them is generally the work that is not in your strength zone, and you are setting them up for failure right out of the gate. When we lead a team, we must build a diverse team of people.

Helping your team understand that their styles and giftings are extremely important in creating the culture you desire is key. Sometimes we have the right people on the bus, as author Jim Collins wrote about in his book, *Good to Great*, but we have them in the wrong seats. I find it interesting that when companies hire people, they invest in them by training them in the tasks of the job. Some even go as far as to do a personality assessment to assess their fit with the team. What they often don't do is a personality assessment to see if they fit the job.

An "I" personality type may be able to do extremely well in an interview, yet if the job is about data, spreadsheets, and working on detailed tasks, they will struggle. They may become disengaged in their work, their performance may suffer, and they will not be happy in the work. Yet, when you hired them, you were so excited that they brought such energy to the team. What happened? They are in the wrong seat on the bus. What do they need every day? Relationships with people, the opportunity to interact with others, and to have fun in the workplace. What might happen if, instead of letting them go, you moved them to a people position in sales, or marketing, and interacting with your customer base?

Understand to Impact

Keep in mind, these are very high-level overviews of DISC® and there are many intricacies that make up and inform each individual person. Part of the journey of life is figuring out our own make up and then being able to understand those around us. As we move on to the next chapter, we will find that all the previous chapters help us meet people where they are to serve them and collectively create impact through generosity.

There is always a fine line, or a caveat, isn't there? Just like there is a fine line between operating with truth and grace, there is a fine line between influence and manipulation. It is necessary to examine our motives to keep a healthy balance so we can continue to lead our teams well.

As a trainer for DISC®, I (Mike) have found it is crucial that the leadership team participates in the training, if you are doing this for your team, and that, as a leader, you set the example by sharing your style. This is huge. Your team's understanding the "why" of DISC®, "being able to work more effectively together," will set your team on a new trajectory.

I was training a Human Resources team in a large organization, and they were highly interested in their colleagues' styles. We do a lot of interactive work in the training, and it can really bring teams across the barriers of people's perceived behaviors. As a part of the training, the participants complete a name badge identifying their style and, as they were at a break and then at lunch, the conversations were all about each other's style.

Someone commented in the groups as part of the feedback after one of our case studies, "It would be nice to know when I go to talk to one of my colleagues what their style is." Someone else suggested they put the style name badge outside their office door or cubical. Everyone bought into the idea. A week or so later, I had the opportunity to drop in, and much to my delight, those name tags with their DISC® style were posted on the office door frames and next to their names in the cubicles. They understood the importance of understanding others to work effectively together.

Understanding personality styles and blends will help you lead people the way they deserve to be led because you can see the different value each can bring to living generously. Just as we learned in the leadership square, some of leadership will be in your wheelhouse and come more naturally to you; other parts will require a bit more intentionality. Meet your people where they are and serve them generously by acting kindly and plentifully, with grace and mercy. Through this, you are building up your emotional intelligence quotient and becoming someone who people want to follow because you connect with them through genuine care. That, my friend, is true generosity.

Questions for Reflection and Discussion

This section of each chapter is to help you think through what you have just read and apply it to your life. As you reflect on what you just read:

1. In what ways did you use TACT² in this last chapter? How will you follow up with those notes?

2. Did you take the DISC® personality style assessment?

    a. If not, I highly encourage you to do so.

    b. If you have, what were the results?

3. What experiences in your life have had the biggest impact on you and your leadership?

4. How does knowing yourself help you to understand others?

5. How can you express generosity through your unique make up (Personality, Gifts, Talents, Strengths, etc.)?

6. By sharing your uniqueness with others, you bless them in ways that come naturally to you. How could you bless someone today?

7. What keeps you from sharing your uniqueness with others? Why?

Chapter 9

INVITE THE GENEROUS PEOPLE

enerosity is evidence of inner transformation, the result of the work God has done and is doing inside an individual. These experiences can change how we think or perceive people and the world around us. Experiences are neither good nor bad. They are only viewed as such through the perspective we have at a given time.

Once upon a time, there was an old farmer who had worked his crops for many years. One day his horse ran away. Upon hearing the news, his neighbors came to visit. "Such bad luck," they said sympathetically, "you must be so sad."

"We'll see," the farmer replied.

The next morning the horse returned, bringing with it two other wild horses. "How wonderful," the neighbors exclaimed! "Not only did your horse return, but you received two more. What great fortune you have!"

"We'll see," answered the farmer.

The following day, his son tried to ride one of the untamed horses, was thrown, and broke his leg. The neighbors again came to offer their sympathy on his misfortune. "Now your son cannot help you with your farming," they said. "What terrible luck you have!"

"We'll see," replied the old farmer.

The following week, military officials came to the village to conscript young men into the army. Seeing that the son's leg was broken, they passed him by. The neighbors congratulated the farmer on how well things had turned out. "Such great news. You must be so happy!"

The man smiled to himself and said once again.

"We'll see,"

A point of view is just that—a view from a point. Personality style also plays a role in how we perceive the experiences around us, as we saw from the last chapter. I think it is important to paint a picture for all of us to understand that we each see the world through the color of the glasses through which we are viewing it. When we understand this, it's a mile marker— a new awareness. It reveals to us that we are hitting the next level of influence. That is, we see in part and others see in part. The full picture can only be experienced through active and full participation with others. When we look at a beach ball, we may see blue and the person directly across from us sees red. While we are both right in saying the ball is either blue or red, if we view it from a higher vantage point, we see that the ball is, in fact, several slices of color.

With this, there are ways for each of us to show up and serve others as we lead them to places of generosity.

Experiences

We went on a hike as a family not that long ago up in the lower foothills of the Cascade Mountains. It was a beautiful, sunny, and warm summer day. We weren't really "hiking" per se; we were more "exploring" that day. We were foraging for berries and edible plants as we moseyed down the trail. We came to an opening where there was a logging road perpendicular to the trail. This crossing was the beginning of another trailhead, and there was a sign with a large map displayed for us to navigate which direction we would go. According to the map, we followed the logging road down into a valley, which appeared to be where they would release dam waters, and which would therefore be flooded occasionally. I wasn't too worried about that because there seemed to be enough plant growth that it didn't seem to be a danger to us.

As we made our way down into the valley on this one-lane logging road, to our right there was a hillside that ran steeply down into the sandy floor below. To our left was a steep incline covered with thick blackberry bushes, except for two game trails that appeared to be well-traveled by a large herd of deer or elk who lived in the area. We continued to look for animal signs as we made our way to the bottom of the ravine. The sandy floor at the base of the valley felt like what I have always imagined the surface of the moon to be like. The dust was thick and fine, almost like drywall dust a few inches deep.

It was easy to spot even the smallest animal prints. There were tracks all over. Deer, elk, raccoon, dog, and rabbit tracks stamped the valley floor and left a bit of history for us to try and piece together. *Where were they going? What were they doing?*

Were they running, walking, or stopping to have a bite to eat? My son and I especially enjoyed trying to figure out this labyrinth of animal life. At least, we did until the situation changed.

The girls were about 100 yards out in front of us, making their way down the trail, when we happened upon a rabbit. Well, half a rabbit, really. It hadn't been gone long. In fact, it appeared that, whatever had killed it, we had likely scared it off as we approached the valley. All the hairs on my neck stood up. I instantly didn't care about animal tracks or answering the questions of what they were doing. My priority became getting out of there! I invited everyone to join me as we cautiously made our way past the half a rabbit and up the trail.

There were a few things that jumped out to me in this experience. One, life is very much like this, where something happens that changes our perspective, and we pivot because of it. Seeing the rabbit changed my understanding of what was going on around me and shifted my priorities immediately. Two, not everyone was aware of it. Jackie and Sophia would have kept walking down the trail and it could have become an even more dangerous situation. And three, inviting everyone along helped them to get to where we needed to go. On the way home, we were able to discuss what had happened and everyone was able to learn a little something about sticking together and being aware of our surroundings.

Our experience in life is made up of moments, moments that create memories and pave neural pathways in our brain that set our subconscious and direct our behaviors, some great and some terrible. Some are challenging moments and others are extremely rewarding. Some honorable and some downright appalling. The sum of these moments and how we perceive them determines the direction of our lives. Like we learned in an earlier chapter, the terror barrier often keeps us from moving forward, but knowing that, it also keeps others from moving forward. However, when we break through the terror barrier, we can see a new perspective with our experiences. By sharing those experiences (let's call them "stories" now), we can help others in their situation. Sharing stories gives us an opportunity to invite other people on a journey and lead them to a better place. It's something we all need.

Connecting with People

"My precious!"

I am sure all of us are now doing the voice in our minds of one of the most famous lines uttered by one of the saddest characters in literary and film history, in my opinion. For 500 years, Gollum was alone, deep in the Misty Mountains, and his thoughts were poisoned by that lonely experience. No one to counter the negativity in his mind. No one to offer any encouragement. Gollum didn't start out that way. He experienced something that pushed him down that path. Greed and murder led to shame and despair. It plagued him throughout the story in *The Lord of the Rings*.

We need relationship with each other in order to be healthy. As we go through life, and the moments that define our stories shape how we see the world, it is essential to do it with others. But there are introverted people who need much more time in solitude than the extroverted people who would go crazy if they couldn't be around others. We all process information differently, so we strive to find common ground. I believe common ground is found in the heart.

Love is a universal language. It crosses cultural boundaries.

Unlocking the heart happens when you gain influence with a person or a group. Gaining influence with a person or group, like we discussed in chapter 4, is all about connecting with them. Relationships are built on moments in time. People who can connect with others understand that it's not just what you say to them, but how you make them feel. Understanding people helps us connect with them better. Here are two truths you can lean on:

All people want to be known.

All people want to be loved.

How do you take those two simple truths and bring them to life? The answer is connection.

People desire to be known, but fear being known because if you knew them—really knew them—you wouldn't love them. This is the cause of Gollum running off to the Misty Mountains and the cause of much of the world's issues as well. But, as we build the bridge to connect with people, we are accepting them for who they are, and loving them through the process of who they are called to be.

Connecting with people is easier for some, but is a worthy endeavor for all of us as a skill that we can develop. Shared experiences and sharing stories allow bonds to develop that will create meaningful connections.

Room Tone

While people desire to be known and loved, these are also two of their greatest fears. We fear being known because if you knew, like, really *knew* the depths of my heart, you wouldn't love me. And if you loved me, I would be setting myself up to be deeply hurt. While these fears and feelings are often not verbally expressed, we sense them each and every day through interactions and conversations.

People can hear your words, but they can feel your attitude. Just like my experience on the trail with my family that day had the hairs on my neck standing on end, we experience the world around us through our senses, thoughts, and spirit. There is an undercurrent of spirituality in everything. Sometimes it can be difficult for us to see or understand because we generally don't talk a lot about it. However, it makes up more of our life than we may realize.

There are two primary reasons I say this. First, because everything you do is based on what you believe to be true. Truth is a spiritual reality that points us in a direction. Second, the spiritual world isn't just "out there." We experience it regularly but are so accustomed to the experience that we don't give it a second thought.

Have you ever walked into a room and immediately know that people who are there were arguing? This is what I call "room tone." This is where the physical world and spiritual world meet. Why can you feel it when people are arguing? I believe it happens for two reasons. First, we are all giving and receiving energy. All the time. Frequency emits in waves as it travels. When a frequency touches our body, our bodies can feel it. Sometimes the frequency feels pleasant, and we like it. Other times, it makes us feel uncomfortable. Secondly, people also pick up on the nuances of our expressions, for example, our facial expressions and body language. The way we hold our-selves in a room. The pauses in our voice as we speak. All of it communicates something and the listener is always picking up these clues to create a fuller picture of what is happening.

I was at a party, my wife walked into the room, and our eyes met. I lit up! Her spirit made my heart sing and when that hap-pens, it shines out of your face! You know, just like the song, "If you're happy and you know it, then your face will surely show it." We met at the entry way of the house, and she embraced me with a warm hug. I could feel her love, happiness, compassion, care, and joy pouring into me, almost like I had dying batteries and had just been plugged in to the wall outlet. To this day, if I am sad, down, or discouraged, I will lay my head on her and she generously gives me some of her energy and it picks me up.

The beliefs, attitudes, and energy we have come out in subtle ways and impact the room tone either positively or negatively. Actors often do this using manipulation. Method acting will allow a character to transform to become like the one they are trying to portray. I am convinced that doing this leads many actors and actresses alike to a depressive state because, like me when I was younger, they are wearing a mask in order to control a situation.

Unnatural Grit

A man's uncle was struck with Gold Fever in the days of the Gold Rush. He set out for the West to stake his claim and strike it rich. He bought a claim and began to labor with a pick and shovel. After weeks of difficult work, he found what he was looking for: gold.

The discovery made it necessary to bring in machinery, to retrieve the gold from the mine and bring it up to the surface. He discreetly covered his discovery and went home to Maryland, where he began to recruit family to help him come up with the money to cover the cost of the expensive machinery he would need. When he got the money, he had the machinery shipped and went back to the mine with his nephew to help work the mine.

His first car full of gold was sent off to the smelter. The payout was proving that they had one of the largest mines in Colorado. After a few more cars full of gold, they would have enough to pay off the debt from the machinery. Then they would be pulling in the cash!

To say they were excited was an understatement! That's when something happened that they didn't expect. The vein of gold flat out disappeared. They drilled and drilled, desperately searching for the vein that was to make them rich, but to no avail.

After some time, they decided to quit. They sold all the equipment to a junk yard and told the junk man their story. This man immediately called in a mining engineer. They went out to the mine and the mining engineer was able to calculate precisely where the vein would be picked up. The original claim owners knew nothing about fault lines, but the engineer calculated that they were three feet away from the vein when they gave up. The junk yard man went right to work and sure enough, they were, in fact, only three feet from gold.

This story illustrates the reality that hits too many. They give up right before they make it big. They quit only three feet from the breakthrough. What they were pushing for was so close, but in their mind, it was too far.

I want to encourage you, right where you are, in whatever you are doing: you never really know when that vein of gold will show up and you never know how close you are to it. Keep pushing forward! Call in an expert when necessary to help push you to where you need to go. When it gets hard, don't give up. Get creative! I call this having a "How can I?" attitude. It is shifting our focus from our problems to our options.

Often, we come to a fork in the road where a decision to quit or keep pushing becomes a tough call. Here's where calling comes into play. The way I see it is this: if you are called to it, keep going. Sometimes we are called to difficult things because of the lessons and the personal development that come along with it. Other times we come to difficult things to help direct us back to the path we are called to. And still others are difficult due to the seeds we have sown that aim to choke us out. Learning to navigate this is life itself: learning how to distinguish the difference between challenges that are meant to keep you *from* your calling and challenges that are meant to push you *toward* your calling.

In the leadership square from chapter 7, we see that adversity is more challenging when it's new. If we have been through it before and we have an idea of how to navigate it, we are more likely to push through the challenge. We see those as opportunities to serve others and grow.

Serve with What You Have

As we navigate the path of life according to our calling, it's not uncommon to compare ourselves to others who may be further along in their journey, and wish to be where they are. We look to people who have been successful and think just how nice it would be to be in that position. What we fail to recognize is that everyone is in a different place in their journey. This causes us to be hard on ourselves, and prevents us from stepping out to serve. We may rationalize:

I don't have time.
I don't know what to say.
I don't have the resources.
I am not qualified.
I don't have any followers.
I have a tough time working with others and inspiring them to do the work.

Take me, for example, writing this book. If I'd chosen to justify my actions with the above comments, this book would have never been finished. It has taken A LOT of time. There were many times in the process that I experienced writer's block or had a difficult time communicating what my brain thought was very clear. It takes many resources to get a book launched. I'm just a regular guy. I don't have a line of people looking to hear what I have to say. I am thankful that I chose to start with what I had—an idea, a concept—and begin building on it. I am thankful that I took the advice of Chris Robinson.

In fact, I think we all need to take the advice of my friend Chris: "Get out the house!" Like I mentioned in chapter 7.

We often get in our own way, but I want to encourage you that your motive to make a difference will inspire action naturally. Your motive to stay comfortable will rob yourself and others of inspiration. Don't waste another minute—get out the house!

Getting out the house takes practice. We tend to want it all to happen at once, but keep in mind that people who have better relationships, are more productive with time, or exhibit patience have had many opportunities to practice these skills. Practice is starting with what you have and serving where you are. Don't give up practicing. The ones who push through and make it a regular habit tend to process the successes and failures they have had and make course corrections, rather than allowing them to become a wall.

Think of someone you look up to, someone who is where you want to be. Just ask them; I guarantee they will have some great stories of how they have overcome some very difficult challenges.

Think about it this way: if the truth about living out of abundance is that relationships take practice and you have spent your life, up to this point, doing things another way, you may have a learning curve ahead of you. Learning to do something differently will take time, patience, commitment, and most certainly graciousness and mercy toward yourself and others. The act of being kind and generous to another, with mercy and grace, begins within you and extends outward from where you are.

You have what it takes, even if it doesn't feel like it. It might just look different in you than it does in someone else. My natural skills and talents don't come naturally to others, or vice-versa. The same is true for your gifts. This took me a long time to realize.

We generally assume others think like we do. We assume the words they say have the same meaning. We assume they are like us. Once I came to the realization that we all see and experience the world differently, I began to feel more free to utilize my own unique skillset to serve others, instead of trying to emulate another person's style. Naturally, I am encouraging, so why not offer someone encouragement? That's an easy win! Do I always do a good job? NO! But I try. "A" for effort, right?

It has been a combination of both practice AND failure that opened the door for me to learn this tough lesson. If I had given up when it got hard, I would never have learned to become who I am today—not perfect, just more mature and further along in the journey, and hopefully more authentic.

This same concept works in business too. When my kids were younger, they wanted to start a business. They decided to set up a lemonade stand—a great first business, if you ask me! I was excited for them. My son was looking up all the equipment and supplies they would need—a table, a tablecloth with their logo, cups, ice, lemonade, a large pitcher, etc. My daughter saw the total and did not want to put in her money because she was intent on *saving it for college*. This was a great opportunity to share this same lesson with them. Start with what you have!

Instead of buying a new table, they could use the card table we already owned. Rather than designing, printing, and ship-ping a tablecloth with their logo, why not use the tablecloth we already had and draw a logo on a piece of paper and tape it to some cardboard? I encouraged them to think creatively: "You could also use the pitcher we have in the kitchen—while not as big as the one you want, you wouldn't have to spend any money out of your pocket."

Some things were necessary to purchase—lemonade, ice, cups, etc. But they got the point: start with what you have, and utilize as much of it as you can in order to get started. That allows you to keep your costs low and gives you the ability to turn a profit instead of paying investors.

START. WITH. WHAT. YOU. HAVE.

Building Community

Building community starts with an invitation. The invitation turns into a relationship and that relationship develops trust. Trust comes when people's words and actions line up. One way to say it is this: to simply do what you say you will do. In this book, we are looking at how generosity can change our lives and the lives of those around us. Well, let me tell you, it can change more than just the lives of people we know! It can transform communities of people—and even has the power to change the world!

But it starts within the heart of one person. That person begins to make changes in their life that reflect generosity. Then, this one person decides they will be a catalyst for generosity in their community. They begin to make changes by asking simple questions like: *How can I get to know them better? How can I show them that I truly love them?*

Trust is built over time and when you value others and spend your energy on building healthy relationships, generosity flows naturally.

I met a gentleman who has had a big impact on my life. Dave Robbs was just a man who happened to live in the same town as me. When Jackie and I opened our café, he was one of the first to see the new look. While we hadn't finished our remodel completely, we held an event with our local Chamber of Commerce to give them a first look. We had developed the space to a place where we felt it would be worthwhile to open the doors.

I remember Dave coming up to me and asking me questions about my plan on a few items, specifically the ceiling tiles. We had an exposed ceiling and I mentioned we planned to keep much of it open, but had to cover the areas where we would be preparing food. Dave asked questions others hadn't.

I would see Dave on a regular basis at Chamber of Commerce events and got to know his passion for helping small businesses in Southern Africa through a non-profit he started, called "The Poyeho Project." He was great at processes, procedures, and planning. These were areas I tend to struggle with, so Dave and I met for coffee.

Dave has an amazing story and was able to coach me through some tough growth periods in my business journey. He has been a mentor, coach, and friend since we opened our café. He came back later with a friend and had coffee in our shop—something he would do regularly for years to come because of the relationship we had built. Dave began bringing his friends, family, and clients in and even more relationships were developed. This is exactly how community forms.

When you see value in another person, your desire for them is not that they would be just like you. Rather, it's for them to be everything God created them to be. Dave recognized that I don't think like he does. He leveraged his experience and insight to help me become better and we both rose because of it.

Everyone has their uniqueness that has been bestowed upon them. They have talents, gifts, and natural abilities that sets them apart from others. Don't equate equality for being the same. Remember, it is about value, not uniformity. Since you have a calling that is a benefit to your community, once you start using it to add value to others, community is something that just happens. The word "community" is derived from the Latin word *communis*. It's the same root word from which we get "communication" and "communion," which means "oneness, union, with, together." Communication leads to communion. Connection leads to community. All three represent a commitment to one another.

As you step out, people who value what you value—and want to be a part of what you are doing and the difference you are making—will show up. You don't have to seek them out first. The journey starts alone, but when you invite others, it will end up collecting a community along the way. Invite them! This community will be looking for you to teach them what it means to live generously along the way. It doesn't have to be a formal education; you don't need to develop fancy speeches; your model is a great starting place. Then, as conversations take place, relationships develop and your methods will develop based on the community you are building and the people you lead.

My guess is you have already started. If not, there is no better time to start than right now. It's always the right time to invite others into a good friendship. After all, we could all use a good, generous, friend.

Questions for Reflection and Discussion

This section of each chapter is to help you think through what you have just read and apply it to your life. As you reflect on what you just read:

1. In what ways did you use TACT[2] in this last chapter? How will you follow up with those notes?

2. Whom is God putting on your heart to invite into something more?

3. What are you inviting them (the people from question 2) into?

4. What unique experiences can you share in your life that would help others?

5. How do you help people know they are known and loved?

6. How can you start with what you have right now?

7. What calling is God putting on your heart that you can't say no to, but is bigger than you?

8. What is holding you back from fulfilling the call on your life?

Chapter 10

GENEROUS PEOPLE, GENEROUS CITY

O ur world is in desperate need. We cannot afford to wait another day to begin living lives committed to adding value to others. Your time is now, and I believe God is calling you to something great!

Desperate Times Call for Intentional Leaders

Look at the world around you. It's clearly hurting. It seems impossible to turn on the television, radio, or the news feeds without seeing and hearing the division and global unrest. It's as though a minute doesn't go by where we aren't reminded of the pain that is felt and how that pain projects into the lives of others. We are all hurting in need of a Savior.

We are living in a day where mass killings are occurring regularly. We are seeing wars take place and hearing rumors of wars as tensions between countries mount. But it isn't just all the big things we see in media; it's also experienced every day in our cities and towns.

It might be something as simple as driving down the road; someone is mad. It could be that you're going too fast. It could be that you're going too slow. It could be that you didn't step on the gas instantly after the light turned green or it could be that you didn't do it at all and were the only one who made it through before the light turned red. We are all in a hurry and don't have time to deal with other people's interference with our day.

People are growing less patient. As the world desperately tries to figure things out on their own, they are missing the simple truth that unlocks the Kingdom on Earth. The world is looking for a Savior. someone who can come in and solve their problems. What we often think and believe is that our problems are "out there."

What does this have to do with living generously? **Living generously is the pathway that God is using to partner with His people to point people to Himself and solve the world's problems.** He knows the world needs a Savior. That's why He sent His Son to live a perfect life and die the death of a criminal, so He could save us. God is not mad at us. He is patiently waiting for us to see just how much He loves us.

The world is hurting because it has been rocked by a long deficit in quality leadership where we have had many leaders pointing people to things to "help." But, in reality, they have been causing more harm than good because they haven't been pointing people to the one thing that would help. These leaders are more afraid of impacting how people feel about *them* than they are in helping them realize that it is the power of God, who raised Jesus from the dead, that can save us!

We are struggling to model something that hasn't yet been observed and trying to do it on our own rather than resting on the finished work. The world desperately needs people who are willing to do hard things and work through the obstacles and trials associated with building genuine leaders. The world needs leaders who recognize the time in which they are called to. The harvest is ripe but the laborers are few. Leaders who understand this reality, and desire to direct—lead, model, teach, equip, and guide—others to wholeness, wholeness that can only come from God alone. John Maxwell penned a wise saying: *a leader is one who knows the way, goes the way, and shows the way.*

Desperate times call for intentional leaders because desperate times also bring out the wolves. Wolves are opportunistic hunters. They use visual cues to show any weakness or vulnerability. Desperation is a reaction to hopelessness. These wolves love desperation because it allows them to come in and lead the flock astray.

Desperation, on the other hand, also shows that there is opportunity. When there is desperation, it shows there is room for hope. It shows that a leader who it ready to make a difference, can show up and do just that—give the people hope.

> "If we don't change the direction we are going, we are likely to end up where we are heading." - Lao Tzu

You are becoming a leader the people around you need. I say "becoming" not because you aren't already leading and making impact, but because we will never truly arrive at our fullest potential. In life, there is no finish line but death. There will always be room for us to grow, another summit to ascend on the mountain. You are developing a generous culture, one in which people can meet each other where they are, but not remain there because you are taking them somewhere—up the mountain.

Masks

If we are to partner in helping to point people to a place where they can be whole, we must first find wholeness and healing for ourselves. Often, we do things through our own willpower rather than relying on strength that God has given. One of the reasons I appreciate DISC® assessments is that while it helps us see ourselves, it really encourages us to live authentically by taking off the masks we wear.

From a young age, most of us become exceptional at wearing masks in various situations, and the longer we wear them the more comfortable they feel. In fact, we get so good at it, and they are so comfortable, that sometimes we don't even realize we are wearing a mask at all. This means we have legitimately forgotten our identity and our unique purpose. And, this becomes a disservice to the world around us.

Masks are our way of hiding the gift of power God has given us to promote another, less powerful, finite power. Why would we trade in a Rolex for a Casio? You are a masterpiece that has been gifted amazing abilities.

What do you do when you get a gift? When you receive it, do you leave it wrapped and stick it in the closet? Or do you unwrap it and show it off to all your friends and family? Your personality is an amazing and unique gift. It is a gift to those around you; it adds value to others, but only if you unwrap it and share it with them.

Too often we try so hard to fit in with the crowd that we fail to showcase our true self for the benefit of others. Too often we are focused on trying to impress others, appease others, avoid judgement, or navigate the assumed expectations others have that we fail to recognize we don't need to wear masks to be appreciated. The gift of you is the very thing that allows you to see things others can't see. It allows you to understand and do things others would struggle with. Your unique gift is the answer to completing the rest of us! You owe it to yourself and others to take off the mask and reveal the gift that is you.

I was in a meeting with two directors of engineering. I was a technician at the time and was invited into a meeting to discuss an issue the engineering department was trying to solve with an optical disc drive. We were in a small conference room, watching a slow-motion video of the mechanical functions inside the device.

After the first time watching the video, I saw the problem, but I didn't say anything. We watched the video several times and I listened to them discuss what they were thinking for over 30 minutes before I spoke up and pointed out what I had seen in the video. It took a lot of courage for me to speak up and I had to talk myself into it. But I learned a valuable lesson that day: we all see things differently and what I may have found simple and obvious is not always obvious to others.

There was a meme I saw a while back of a cat in a carrying case. The cat was staring at the door, wanting to get out of the case. What the picture revealed was that the top of the case had been taken off and, while the cat could have easily escaped, it was too focused on the way it thought it had to be done—through the door. Circumstances, situations, mindset, physical and emotional health, personality styles, etc. all play into how we see things. No one expects perfection from others, but often we expect it from ourselves.

Learning to take off a mask is hard. It means being authentic. It means showing our strengths and our weaknesses, revealing shame for things of the past, and wrestling with our pride. In society, there is not an emphasis on being authentic. There is an underlying and unspoken culture that tells us quite the opposite. A child plays with a toy and another child takes it from them; the response is to address the behavior by saying something like, "You can't take things from people's hands." While a good truth—stealing is wrong—it doesn't address the root of the problem. We all feel like the world either does or should revolve around us at times, but choosing to not give into that temptation is where the real power lies. When we correct behavioral problems, we must reassure others that it is normal to experience those thoughts and feelings. What we want to do is recognize that we are thinking and feeling those things, and ask ourselves why and what should we do about it.

We live in a society that has spent decades trying to make people live moral lives by correcting behavioral issues, but ultimately causing feelings of shame and rejection to be covered with masks. This challenges the ability to have intimate relationships, and eliminates self-confidence.

As a young man, I would often find myself trying to please other people to get them to like me—doing funny and sometime dangerous things, like diving headfirst out a first-floor window to impress others and get them to laugh. While I didn't understand why I did those things at the time, that's exactly what I was doing. I became so focused on attention seeking from others that I began to lose my identity in it.

If you are not authentic, you will never be able to lead others in a healthy way. We can only lead people to places we have been ourselves.

Lead Them Well

There is a great responsibility to leadership. This is why I believe generosity is so important for leaders to understand, and one of my primary reasons for writing this book. When we recognize the weight of this responsibility, it can do one of two things: either it will compel us to press forward in faith or it will cause us to turn and run in fear.

I was operating in the latter most of my life. I was fearful because I didn't want the responsibility and weight that came with leadership. I didn't want to be accountable for what I did and said. In fact, I would avoid it at all costs until I realized that, by not leading, it was as if I were walking past a wounded person with a first-aid kit, completely selfish and self-serving. The good news is, I have had my eyes opened to new realities that have helped me lead in my community.

Not all leaders are created equal, as I am sure you have come to realize over the course of your life so far. As we have discussed throughout this book, everyone is a leader. How you use your influence is what matters. I believe there are generous people everywhere. If you're having a hard time finding one, be one!

The influence you have in the lives of others is a gift from above. You were created, uniquely, to do the work and create opportunities to invite others into a vision for something better through generosity. The impact you have starts right where you are with what you have. You don't need to be the president of a country or a CEO of an organization to make an impact. You just have to be you and steward well what you have been given.

Some of the most impactful things you will ever do is to treat your parents, siblings, spouse, children, friends, and neighbors with generosity. Great leaders don't just want the best *from* you; they want the best *for* you. Great leaders will pursue your well-being and continue to encourage you to reach your potential as they model, teach, equip, and guide you along the way.

As a leader, you are creating opportunities for your followers to operate in an environment where they can be authentic and grow. When I said I would coach my son's soccer team, I had no idea what I was signing up for. I didn't know the rules of soccer or the basics. However, I was committed to investing time to help those kids learn something more important than how to play the game: the character needed to work together.

As you create opportunities for people to grow, it creates opportunities for them to have real impact. People desire to belong and do something significant. They want their life to have meaning. This, unfortunately, has been used to cause great harm to people and has broken trust by leaders trying to manipulate them. In order to do this successfully, your followers not only need to know you are trustworthy; they need to experience your trustworthiness for themselves. It is one thing to know *about* someone and another altogether to *know* them.

All people want to be helped, not sold. Help them get what they want and need. In turn, they will help you get what you want.

Transformed Communities

Community is transformed by people who desire to make a difference with others who desire to do the same. These leaders commit to living out good values that translate into action. In the book *Change Your World,* Rob Hoskins shares a framework he developed for ensuring that no matter the problem to be resolved, the issue to be addressed, or the circumstance to be transformed, there is a clear path. He calls this process the Five D's:

Discover – Find out what's really going on and who is doing something about it.

Design – Develop a strategy that begins with the end in mind and builds on your strengths, not your weaknesses.

Deploy – Implement your plan. Start small, fail soon, and adjust often.

Document – Measure to make sure that your intended outcomes are being accomplished.

Dream – Start the cycle all over, expanding what works and abandoning what doesn't.

You see, transformation to a generous culture starts with a dream, just like all great things do. We see a better future for ourselves and others. This desire to make a dream a reality, a difference in the world around us, is what launches us forward into the fog and propels us through the unknown.

> "We can have the intent to love others, but without initiative, without real acts of respect, caring, and affection for another, intention remains useless, soulless. Thinking is not love– giving is. - Brendon Burchard

Many in the world recognize that there is room for improvement and wish someone would come along to make it better. The difference between them and you is your commitment to taking action through good values and a desire to make a difference with other difference makers. This work is not fast. It can be, but I have found it is built at the speed of relationship. At times it will grow quickly, but it will grow only as quickly as it can for genuine relationship to blossom.

Don't rush. As you go, continue to take the next right step. What you are doing is way more impactful than you may realize. Motivate others to action and see the dream of a better tomorrow come to life because you said yes to the call.

"To the world you may only be one person, but to one person you may be the world." - Dr. Seuss

Generosity transforms communities through daily modeling: building, encouraging, equipping, teaching, and empowering other leaders who want to make a difference. Only when you lead well in the small things will new opportunities find you and take you to new heights. Don't be limited to thinking that leading yourself well is any less important than leading an organization of 100,000 people. It is equally as important.

When you are faithful to fulfill what you have been called to *now*, your calling will expand to reach beyond what you thought it could. You will be amazed at what God will do to a faithful and obedient follower. Generous people take what they have been given to steward and transform the culture into generous families, businesses, towns, communities, cities, countries, and beyond.

Generosity Inside Out

Walking home in the rain sucks. It's even worse when there are no sidewalks and you have to navigate the muddy pathways along a busy road and it's cold. This was a random day in March of 2002. I was in the ninth grade in Washington State. It was grey and it was cold.

As I traversed the slippery trail and managed to stay on my feet on my way home from school, a car sped past me and swerved into a mud puddle and sprayed me with muddy water. I was furious! Earlier that day, two of my teachers had given me a hard time because of some unexcused absences. I mean, who had really missed me for the previous nine days? I didn't open up to most of my friends, let alone tell a teacher, what was going on in my life. After all, it was a mess and seemed to be falling apart even more.

I particularly remember thinking how frustrated I was this day, even before the mud shower.

As if I weren't cold and wet enough, now I was muddy. Needless to say, I was angry. Mad that someone would add to an already bad day with another irritating circumstance. *Why me?* I grumbled.

Most kids experience feelings like this, especially in junior high and high school. My overall situation was a little different than most. Earlier that school year was 9/11, where our country experienced something that had never happened before. It was scary. A few months later, and just two days before Christmas, I found out my dad had passed away in a motorcycle accident.

It was a confusing time for me. I was hurting inside. I felt like the world was actively against me, trying to break me down.

Nothing was going my way. I felt lost. I often thought the world would be better off if I wasn't in it.

Then I heard a story of generosity that changed my life forever—a story of a Man who sacrificed everything for me, a lonely kid in Puyallup. A story of Someone who cared. Who loved me not for what I could do, but simply for who I was.

It was then that I began to see something different. While it wasn't until much later that I realized what God had started in me that Easter, I recognize the profound impact this moment had on the journey.

Just like I was, the world around us is hurting. People walk around with wounds they don't share. We pass by them every day and we all pretend that everything is okay inside. We take them at their word when they say, "I'm fine, you?" Like they are being honest. Ha!

My eyes were opened not only to that truth, but also to the truth that love heals. Love has power to soften our rough edges. Applying generosity: being kind and plentiful with grace and mercy isn't always easy.

I didn't change overnight. But a seed was planted. Something began to grow. That was the seed of generosity that began to blossom. Because He was generous, I can be.

Generosity is the tone in your voice that shows you actually care to have someone truthfully answer the question, "How are you today?" It's the way you listen to someone that tells them they matter. It's the time spent preparing a meal for your family. It's the way you model your life for others to follow. Generosity is the ultimate quality of a leader, to be kind and giving to others with grace and mercy. I strive for this quality of abundance daily because it is one I believe can change the world.

There is hope for the world. There is hope for you. Because generosity is contagious.

Someone in the world right now is counting on you to become the best, most generous version of yourself you can be and reveal a love only God can give.

> "Real and lasting changes isn't behavior modification but spiritual transformation." - Craig Groeschel

Join the Generous Movement

Are you ready to make a difference? Generosity is changing lives all over the planet and it is saving people from the grips of fear, abandonment, scarcity, rejection, pain, insecurity, shame, and even death. This work is weighty and lifelong. It requires faith to step out into the unknown to be a difference maker. It requires us to work through our brokenness and embrace those around us by being kind and plentiful with mercy and grace. I believe you were made for such a time as this! Let this be the call to live generously and lead generously to build a culture and community of Generous People.

I am committed to helping to equip people, just like you, to lead by becoming bigger on the inside so you can make a significant, positive, impact in your community and beyond. I want you to join the movement of Generous Influencers and become the leader you were born to be. The goal is to not only train you but offer you helpful resources along the way in a community of people who are doing it, just like you. Head over to the website below and see how you can become a Generous Influencer.

Let's spread hope, love, and generosity, together! And remember, generosity is contagious!

Visit:

www.robertjkaelin.com

Questions for Reflection and Discussion

This section of each chapter is to help you think through what you have just read and apply it to your life. As you reflect on what you just read:

1. What stood out to you in this chapter?
2. In what ways did you use TACT[2] in this last chapter? How will you follow up with those notes?
3. How do you personally see the desperation of the world in its need for healing?
4. How have you been healed? Who needs to hear that story?
5. How can you leverage the concept of the 5 Ds:
   a. Discover
   b. Design
   c. Deploy
   d. Document
   e. Dream
6. How have you seen a leadership deficit in your life?
7. How can you become the leader you needed in your life?
8. What is your next step?

SCAN ME

DISC RESOURCES

ABOUT THE AUTHOR

Robert Kaelin is a visionary leader and the founder of Counter Culture Leadership, a values based organization which helps equip leaders reach their full potential so they can change the world with positive impact, and Generous Influencers, a nonprofit on mission to influence communities with generosity through community events and building relationships. Robert began his journey as an author, speaker, entrepreneur, trainer, and coach after graduating with a Bachelor of Arts in Leadership from Faith International University. He and his wife are also the owners and operators of a café where they implement their mission of leadership training and generosity, and stay involved in their local community.

As a young child, Robert moved to Puyallup, Washington, where he now resides, and discovered his family had deep roots and impact in this city he would come to call home. "Puyallup," a Native American word from the Puyallup tribe, is translated as "the land of the generous and welcoming to all." Desiring to be the change he wanted to see, Robert realized his own personal growth journey was the one he needed to focus on.

For years, Robert thought he was called to be a pastor, but God had other plans and he began a journey in business. Since then, he has been awarded the "Champion of Commerce" award for his work in the city, "Community Builder" Award, and his café has become the "best office outside of the office" as he has continued to show up and serve those around him with the generosity he talks about in this work.

Robert enjoys life in the Pacific Northwest with his wife, Jackie. They have three children and love spending their time with others, adventuring and soaking in the world around them. *Generous Influencers* is Robert's first book.

www.robertjkaelin.com

ENDNOTES

1   "Personal Debt in the U.S.— Statistics & Facts." Statista. com. https://www.statista.com/topics/1203/person-al-debt/#dossierKeyfigures. Accessed February 27, 2023.

2   Carly Hallman. "The Median Debt of Americans." Title-max.com. https://www.titlemax.com/discovery-center/money-finance/the-median-debt-of-americans/. Accessed February 27, 2023.

3   Verma, Prakhar. "Destroy Negativity from Your Mind with This Simple Exercise." Medium.com. https://medium.com/the-mission/a-practical-hack-to-combat-negative-thoughts-in-2-minutes-or-less-cc3d1bddb3af#:~:text=According%20to%20the%20National%20Science%20Founda-tion%2C%20an%20average,negative%20way%20more%20than%20we%20think%20positive%20thoughts. November 27, 2017.

4   Kuhn, Sharfreena and Rieger, Ulrich M. "Health is a state of complete physical, mental and social well-being and not

merely absence of disease or infirmity." https://pubmed.
ncbi.nlm.nih.gov/28389194/. February 3, 2017.

5   Maxwell, John. Everyone Communicates, Few Connect.
Thomas Nelson Incorporated, 2010.

6   Matthew 7:4-5

7   Evans, Tony, and Jonathan Evans. Kingdom Family Devo-
tional 52 Weeks of Growing Together. Colorado Springs:
Focus on the Family Publishing, 2017.

8   Proverbs 29:18

9   Maxwell, John C., and Jim Dornan. Becoming a Person of
Influence: How to Positively Impact the Lives of Others.
Nashville, TN: Harper Collins Leadership, 2018.

10 Tolkien J R R., et al. The Lord of the Rings. London: Harp-
erCollinsPublishers, 2014.

11 "Generosity Comes More Naturally to Some People Than
Others. Here's Why." John Templeton Foundation. https://
www.templeton.org/news/generosity-comes-more-
naturally-to-some-people-than-others-heres-why. Accessed
February 27, 2023.

A free ebook edition
is available with the
purchase of this book.

To claim your free ebook edition:

1. Visit MorganJamesBOGO.com
2. Sign your name CLEARLY in the space
3. Complete the form and submit a photo of
   the entire copyright page
4. You or your friend can download the ebook
   to your preferred device

Print & Digital Together Forever.

Snap a photo   Free ebook   Read anywhere

Printed in the USA
CPSIA information can be obtained
at www.ICGtesting.com
JSHW081726201023
50582JS00002B/23